5 Conversations

How to transform trust, engagement
and performance at work

NICK COWLEY & NIGEL PURSE

WITH LYNN ALLISON

5 Conversations

First published in 2014 by

Panoma Press
48 St Vincent Drive, St Albans, Herts, AL1 5SJ, UK

info@panomapress.com   www.panomapress.com

Book layout by Neil Coe

Printed on acid-free paper from managed forests.

ISBN 978-1-909623-71-2

Praise for *5 Conversations*

"The principles behind 5 Conversations are exactly the same as those applied in the British Olympic Rowing Team to help us build strong teams and win Olympic Gold medals."

**Steve Williams OBE,
double Olympic Gold medallist**

"This is a crucial and absolutely practical book. It understands the nature of how vital the attachment emotion of trust is in organisations, without which no leader can engage the energies of the best people pulling in the same direction."

**Professor Paul Brown, previously Visiting Professor in Organisational Neuroscience,
London South Bank University and in Individual and Organisational Psychology, Nottingham Law School**

"The saying goes "you come into the world alone, you leave this world alone", but in between, 5 Conversations can help you build great relationships in work and life."

Rupert Hodges, Director Leadership Development, BP plc

"If you are genuinely interested in creating a more engaged workforce, this book is a must-read. 5 conversations is chock-full of pragmatic examples that both inform and instruct."

Benson Smith, Chairman,
President & CEO, Teleflex Inc.

"For too long we have compartmentalised our work relationships and ignored our basic humanity in the workplace – this book has reminded us of the importance of these relationships and the conversations that develop them."

Richard Flint, Managing Director,
Sky Bet

"Highly readable, practical and relevant for public and private sectors alike, 5 Conversations draws us back to the origins of communication and teaches us the simple power of honest and authentic conversations for driving organisational engagement and performance. Read this book, and never fear a sabre-toothed tiger again."

Hugh Elliott, Director of Communication,
Foreign and Commonwealth Office

"You would struggle to find conversations that are more important than those that are so expertly explored in this book. 5 Conversations offers a powerful and practical set of strategies for getting to the heart of workplace performance."

Robin Ryde, business author

"5 Conversations demonstrates not only the power that quality conversations can have in the professional workspace for leaders, peers and employees alike – but also how much personal confidence and satisfaction can be gained from the art of good conversation – something that can be easily lost in our era of mobile, email and internet."

Kirsten Cox, Director EMEA Marketing, VMware

"Who said that the art of conversation is dead? This excellent book explains the value of building trusting relationships in order to forge genuine engagement within an organisation."

Tim Williams, HR Director, Pearson UK

"This book is a great idea. It is the first time I've seen very simple and so powerful things said about management: talking about "simply being human" or about "courage" and "curiosity about others", which brings us back to what management really is: interaction between human beings! Something that most managers have a tendency to forget!"

Laurent Camus, Directeur de la Formation, MBDA

"Much of this book really resonates with how we operate – leadership is THE key enabler for success. This book is a practical guide for leaders in how they can evolve and develop the skills and approaches necessary for personal and organisational success."

John Devall, Water Director, Northumbrian Water

"The best is always simple – here are THE 5 conversations we all need to be having at work and probably also at home!"

Robert Rigby-Hall, Chief Human Resources Officer, NXP Semiconductors

"This book takes the power of conversations to new possibilities and it offers valuable and practical tools, ideas and illuminating examples."

Anushia Reddy, VP Global Talent and Organisation Development, Tate & Lyle

"A conversation is an investment in someone's time so why wouldn't you take time to learn how to make the most of that investment? The beauty of this book is, it takes an everyday activity and with a few simple tricks suddenly turns that activity into a powerful motivational tool and it has tips that can be applied in writing as well."

Eleanor Tweddell, Head of Internal Communications, Vodafone UK

Acknowledgements

We would very much like to acknowledge the help and support of all of our colleagues and clients at The Oxford Group who have encouraged us in developing *5 Conversations* and provided examples of the true power of conversation in building relationships and improving business performance.

We would especially like to acknowledge our colleagues Clive Barrow, Olivier Herold, Maggie Matthews, Sheena Porter, Chris Street, Gill Webb and Lisa Williams for their constant encouragement and help in refining *5 Conversations*; Claire Foster for her significant contribution to the development of the *5 Conversations* programme; James Marshall, Janine Schindler and Debbie Wilkes for their professionalism and enthusiasm in working with clients on the programme; our consultants worldwide, in particular Tessa Bradon, Jennifer Cramb, Julie Havard, Jenny Howard, Caro Kingsnorth, Robert-Charles Kahn, Judy Knight, Anne Merland, Robin Ryde, David Seow and Nancy Wang for providing advice and feedback on *5 Conversations* at various stages in its development and for sharing real stories of how *5 Conversations* has made a difference to clients; our colleagues across The Oxford Group for their expertise and patience in setting up support processes for *5 Conversations*, in particular Jenny Greenway and Katrina Strathearn; our clients who have been so generous in giving us their time to attend pilot workshops or review various drafts of this book – their feedback has been invaluable: Laurent Camus, Kate Dee, Bruno de Lacroix, John Devall,

Alison Dubbins, Hugh Elliott, Chelsea Foxwell, Noel Hadden, Chantal Hicks, Paul Iredale, David Kay, Helen Lancaster, Sally McNab, Iain Lobban, Anna Markovits, Adrian Osbourn, Ruth Owen, Eleanor Tweddell, Steve Williams and Tim Williams; and finally Nina Griffiths for reviewing and editing our various drafts and Lynn Allison for creating the framework for this book.

You have helped us bring *5 Conversations* to life – thank you!

Foreword

At the heart of the economic challenge is the uncomfortable truth that – although there is significant variation by country and by organisation – typically only one third of our people are engaged at work, offering most, or all, of their capability and potential. It is self-evident that we need to have many more of our people offering much more of their capability if we are going to compete and to be able to offer the standard of living to which we aspire, and the public services we require. In addition, people's expectations of how they should be treated at work are changing. We no longer automatically defer to our managers and leaders. People have been educated to expect their voice to be heard. The way employees are treated at work will be central to meeting these expectations and therefore to engaging our people.

The 'Engaging for Success Report' that Nita Clarke and I wrote in 2009 for the Department of Business Innovation & Skills drew the evidence together that there is a very clear correlation between levels of engagement and organisational performance. This evidence has been built on by a number of organisations including Bath Business School which proved the link between employee engagement and organisation performance in their seminal paper entitled 'Nailing the Evidence'.

In our Report to Government we outlined the four key enablers of higher levels of employee engagement:

- Visible empowering leadership providing a strong strategic narrative about the organisation, where it has come from and where it aspires to go.

- Engaging managers who focus their people and give them scope, who treat their people as individuals and who coach and stretch their people.

- Employee voice throughout the organisation for reinforcing and challenging views between functions and externally; employees seen as central to the solutions.

- Organisational integrity where the values on the wall are reflected in day-to-day behaviours and where there is no 'say - do' gap.

These four enablers offer, at the broadest level, a way of thinking about employee engagement. The challenge for organisations is to determine what practical actions to take in order to put these enablers in place, and increasingly they are recognising the key role of the line manager in engagement through the relationships they build with their teams.

What this book does well is to identify the five conversations that engaging managers use in order to build deeper more trusting relationships with members of their teams at work. It makes a compelling case for the importance of having these conversations and harnesses the latest evidence from neuroscience on how effective conversations, held with honesty and openness, contribute to building more trusting relationships and how trust underpins productivity and performance.

There are no quick fixes but with time, attention and consistency, leaders can use these conversations to develop habits which will result in productive workplaces, bringing with them higher levels of employee well-being and sustainable economic performance – which benefits us all.

David MacLeod OBE

Co-chair of Engage for Success Task Force

June 2014

Preface

Over the past 30 years we have been privileged to work at The Oxford Group in partnership with many of the world's leading global organisations. Our mission has been to partner with them to develop the skills, behaviours and confidence of their existing and future leadership teams.

For almost the whole of that period our compelling proposition has been a focus on custom-designing unique, tailored solutions that meet the precise requirements of each organisation, often adapted for local language and local delivery around the world, working in close partnership with each client.

This book represents a new departure for us. Over the past five years many prospective and existing clients have challenged us to tell them what we are best at. They have asked us, "What's your signature programme?", "Where do you have a truly world-class offer?", "What's the unique area of learning where you have something that sets you apart?"

This really got us thinking. Up to then we had chosen to define our USP (Unique Selling Proposition) as designing and delivering bespoke, global learning solutions across the whole gamut of the leadership spectrum.

Could we and should we identify a specific area of learning that defined the soul of the company, and which everyone associated with our business would be proud to adopt?

In the end it didn't take us long to answer that question. Perhaps we had always known what our signature offer really was.

Over the years we have designed and run countless programmes to enable leaders to hold more authentic and open, two-way conversations with members of their teams, with the objective of building truly trusting relationships. We have always known instinctively that these trusting relationships are at the heart of getting things done at work, of delivering quality and service to customers. Sometimes the programmes have been called just that – Building Trusting Relationships – but even when the subject has been about Performance Management or Coaching Skills, what we have chosen to focus on has been the quality of the conversation and the relationship rather than the process or the paperwork. Our mantra has always been "the spirit, not the process".

The real breakthrough came when we reviewed one of the best programmes we have ever run. It was designed for the global pharmaceutical business AstraZeneca. Called "Constructive Conversations", AstraZeneca themselves had identified specific conversations that leaders in their R&D functions worldwide needed to have, in order to deepen engagement and therefore improve performance in drug development. This highly successful programme had outstanding feedback and some of the best evaluation results we had ever achieved at that time. We were even able to correlate uplifts in employee engagement amongst the teams whose managers had attended the programme, by comparison with teams whose managers hadn't.

So in 2013 we decided to take the best elements of this programme and then enhance them with what we've observed and learned from working with a wide range of global companies. We've also included insights from neuroscience, used in our Executive Coaching practice, on how trust is built or undermined.

The outcome is this book, and a new workshop, called *5 Conversations to Transform Trust and Engagement at Work*.

We don't think there's anything else out there that goes quite to the heart of how managers and leaders can build trusting relationships at work, explains why it matters in such compelling terms and provides practical advice on how to do it.

And the reason that we say this is that the 5 Conversations programme is a much deeper and richer experience than a conventional skills workshop. It's about helping leaders to develop a deep emotional commitment to holding conversations by trying them out, feeling their power, and believing in their effectiveness – and as a result returning to work with a genuine action plan.

We are receiving outstanding feedback from our clients about the programme and we're in discussions with many of them about adopting it as a core part of the way they deepen engagement or embed a new culture and values. One of our clients said "We've just rolled out our new values worldwide, and these conversations are exactly what we need our leaders to be role modelling in order to embed these values."

This book is our way of sharing this information with you, whether you can attend a 5 Conversations workshop or not. With this book, you can try 5 Conversations yourself. We show you why each conversation is important, how to invite people to have a conversation, examples of what to say and a structure for the interaction.

There is overwhelming academic and empirical evidence that employee engagement is critical to business success. But many commentators stop there and offer only generalised, organisational-level solutions such as communication plans, roadshows or team briefings. In this book we go further by making concrete, practical recommendations for what you can do as an individual to build deeper levels of engagement. For the first time here, we offer you insights into the five key conversations *you* can use at work to deepen engagement and build trust.

Nick Cowley and Nigel Purse

The Oxford Group, June 2014

Contents

CHAPTER 1

Leadership *is* relationship

A Fortune 500 company in the financial services sector recently hired Robert, a senior executive with a competitor, with the deliberate intention of appointing him the successor to a long-standing and successful CEO. Robert had been the number two in his old business and was widely respected in the sector for being a shrewd and technically-savvy operator. This was his big chance to step up. His role was to run a major part of the business over a two-year period to learn the ropes so that he would be ready to step into the existing CEO's shoes at the end of that period. Analysts, investors and commentators were informed of the plan, and the organisation lined up behind the CEO and his new hire to make it happen.

As the two-year deadline approached, staff and commentators alike were astounded to learn that Robert had resigned to move into another operational role with a competitor. The CEO was embarrassed to have lost his successor. Analysts marked the business down and the stock price dipped. What went wrong?

We had the opportunity to talk with a number of senior executives who were working in the business over the two-year period and their observations are telling. Robert moved into his office on the C-suite level of a tower block in Canary Wharf in London's Docklands Development. He put in place an infrastructure of processes, reports and regular meetings in order to manage his part of the business. He published his vision for the future of the business and defined the values it would stand for. He had meetings with customers and analysts. He was diligent, efficient and business-like, turning up for work early every morning and working late into the evening. But within a few months a key member of his team left to join a competitor, and then another and a third found a transfer into another part of the business. Performance dipped and several other key individuals left or made it clear internally they were looking to move. What was happening?

This is what some executives from the business told us:

"We couldn't work for him. It was just too hard. You never knew where you were with him. One day he would be charming and warm; the next he would cut you off at the knees in a meeting. He never left his office or walked round the business and talked to people. It was impossible to build a relationship with him. We never once had discussions about our development or personal goals. It was all transactional – just about the business and the performance targets. It just stopped being any fun. There's only so long that you can take this. The best people in his team simply walked. Why would you put yourself through that when you don't have to? In the end the CEO realised Robert had zero credibility as his successor and they agreed he would resign and they would manage it as an amicable departure, but no one is really under any illusion as to what has actually happened."

In so many organisations today, leaders seem to have forgotten (or never learnt) the power and importance of being simply human – of building personal trusting relationships with those they lead, of listening to others with care and humanity, of making things happen through deep emotional engagement with the people in their teams.

How is leadership changing?

As we approach the third decade of the 21st century we believe there is now compelling evidence that we also need to enter a new era of leadership where the requirement for leaders to build and maintain genuinely trusting relationships with those they lead takes centre stage.

Hold on a moment. Haven't relationships always been at the heart of effective leadership? Yes they have, in the sense that the best leaders have known this instinctively.

However, our observation is that in most organisations today, and for many leaders, relationship building is still seen as an optional extra – a "nice to have" feature rather than an essential component of effective leadership performance. Why do we say this? Because it's only in the last decade that we have had clear evidence that people's engagement at work correlates directly with the quality of the relationship they have with their line manager – and that there is a clear link between people's engagement and the performance of their organisation.

And as this evidence has emerged, so some organisations have started to focus on the quality of leaders' relationships with their people as a critical factor in organisational performance. And some have even gone further, setting explicit expectations of leaders that building and sustaining trusting relationships is a key part of their role, and showing them how to do it. And we've been fortunate enough to have witnessed this at first hand and partnered with some of these organisations to develop a new approach that makes it a reality.

But still in many organisations the idea that a leader can and should be working proactively to build trusting relationships with members of their team as a central, even fundamental, part of the job is either off their radar or actively rejected. Many organisations still promote a very different approach where leaders are expected to be visionary, decisive, compelling individuals who achieve results through drive and force of personality. Whether they have trusting relationships with their people is practically irrelevant. In some cases they will, in other cases they won't. Whether they do or not has little to do with what is expected of them as leaders. Further evidence for this view exists in the competency frameworks and leadership curriculum in many organisations where the quality of leaders' relationships with their people is either absent or hardly features.

Indeed a school of thought still exists that leaders should not get "too close" to their people, for fear of undermining their authority. We have even recently heard the outdated view advocated that effective leaders "keep people on their toes by instilling a bit of fear and uncertainty". In today's world of work where intellectual capital is key and where you need people to bring their intelligence, creativity, passion and commitment to their work, such an approach is doomed to failure. Indeed we argue this is a deeply unhelpful view of what effective leadership looks like. This view is reinforced by the findings of Jim Collins in *Good to Great* [1] where a key factor in building a great organisation was the presence of a "Level 5" leader, who "builds enduring greatness through a paradoxical combination of personal humility plus professional will".

In today's world of work people's expectations of how they will be treated, and how they will be talked to, have changed profoundly. In his book *Never Mind the Bosses: Hastening the Death of Deference for Business Success* [2], Robin Ryde argues:

"The way we talk to one another in organisations is a critical differentiator of success... Managers and leaders cast long shadows and they introduce patterns of discourse that give permission for others to adopt the same habits... It is through an adult-to-adult discourse that we might properly and appropriately confront the issues that need to be addressed in business so we can avoid the negative and divisive consequences of allowing issues to fester and blame to grow. The quality of conversation we engage in could not be more important in the modern age."

We want to convince you that working to build trusting relationships is your first and most profound duty as a leader. When you have trusting relationships with the people in your team, anything is possible; when trust is absent, little of long-term, sustainable value can be achieved.

We will also argue that it *is possible* to work at, practise and become better at building effective, trusting relationships by re-discovering a fundamental truth – the power of honest, authentic, two-way human conversations at work. We will argue that throughout human history people have talked to each other – using gesture and touch, smiles and frowns, myths and stories – to build collaboration and trust and get things done. Somehow in today's world of technology, email, social media, remote working and globalisation we have forgotten this simple truth. As human beings, relationships matter deeply to us. We can't function effectively without them and that applies just as much at work as it does at home. And the quality of the relationship you have with your line manager at work is crucial to your performance and willingness to go the extra mile – whether you sit in the same office as your manager or in a different country.

Leadership and Relationships

In our work over the past decade we have seen two new ideas emerge that taken together will have a profound effect on what passes for excellence in leadership. The first concerns what effective leaders do, the second why and how they do it.

First, there is overwhelming evidence from academic research, government investigation and professionals working in the field, that when employees have high levels of engagement this has a significant, measurable and transformational impact on organisational performance. And the research also shows that it is the quality of the relationship people feel they have with their immediate leader or manager that is the primary driver of these feelings of engagement. So relationships really matter. They are not an optional, take it or leave it factor. They are a fundamental enabler of your and your organisation's ability to attract, keep and get the very best out of your people. **Leadership *is* relationship. No relationship – no leadership.** Leadership is about the trust, stewardship, concern, understanding and humanity you demonstrate towards those whom you lead. If you can build such relationships, add value to people's lives, enable them to flourish and grow, you will earn their loyalty, trust and lasting commitment.

As global research organisation Gallup [3] says, "How employees feel about their job starts and ends with their direct supervisor. If employees feel, among other things, that their supervisor takes a real interest in their development, or offers frequent praise and recognition, they are very likely to be engaged. If companies throughout your country hire the right people to lead and actively encourage the engagement of their workforces, economic dominance will be sure to follow."

And it's not just research into employee engagement which emphasises the importance of building relationships. The latest evidence from the growing field of neuroscience also shows why the type of conversations you have with others and how you approach them has a fundamental effect on their behaviour and work performance.

Secondly, how do effective leaders build trusting relationships? We now know that effective leaders use authentic, two-way human conversations to build trusting, productive relationships with team members and others around them. Building these conversations into your daily life at work (and beyond) will not only make you a more effective and productive leader, but will also give you a deep sense of fulfilment and enhanced quality of life. No longer is it the case that the quality of the relationships you have at work is something random or mysterious. There is growing evidence that, whether you are an introvert or an extrovert, a technical expert or a generalist, a sales executive or an accountant, you can deepen your relationships by consciously building these key conversations into every day of your working life.

And the real beauty of this finding is that you don't have to be slick, word perfect, or a great conversationalist for this to work. You just have to be authentic – to enter each conversation with the genuine intention of more deeply understanding your colleague, showing care and stewardship, and providing support and encouragement.

What are the key conversations effective leaders use?

Through our work with thousands of leaders in hundreds of organisations around the world we have identified the five critical conversations that the most effective leaders use to build and sustain trusting relationships. These are:

1. **Establishing a trusting relationship** – a conversation with a team member to share a deep, mutual understanding of your respective drivers, preferences, motivators and de-motivators for high performance at work, and to understand what makes each other tick

2. **Agreeing mutual expectations** – a conversation about not only what you are both trying to achieve at work, but also why, and the expectations you can have to support each other in achieving these outcomes

3. **Showing genuine appreciation** – a conversation to help a team member focus on where they are being successful, to jointly understand the reasons for their success, to say how much you appreciate their contribution and to find further ways in which they can deploy their skills and talents to benefit both themselves and the organisation

4. **Challenging unhelpful behaviour** – a conversation to agree a new and more effective set of behaviours when what a team member or colleague is saying or doing is getting in the way of team performance

5. **Building for the future** – a conversation to explore the future career aspirations of a team member and give you the best possible chance of creating conditions that will enable them to build that future career within your organisation rather than elsewhere

You may feel these conversations sound simple and obvious and perhaps they are. But every leader we talk to agrees with this fundamental observation – *that in today's world of work they simply don't happen* – either enough or at all.

To get you started we will give you a structure for each conversation, sample questions and ideas, and a format to follow. But – even if you stumble over your words, or forget a specific question, or end up off track – they work anyway because what people detect and respond to is your genuine intention to make a connection, to be interested in them as a fellow human being, to reach out.

Of course, the conversations aren't linear, following one after the other mechanistically. The most effective leaders have internalised them and move smoothly from one to the next throughout their working day. And they aren't seen as additional conversations to be added to an already busy schedule, but rather as an even more effective way to use regular catch-up and review sessions.

Contrast these conversations with the old, top-down model of business communication. Today's employees question their employers and are not prepared to be passive recipients of information. In a Harvard Business Review article, "Leadership is a conversation" [4], Groysberg and Slind describe the new reality of leadership communication as having a number of drivers, including:

1. Generational change – as millennials and other younger workers are becoming a greater proportion of the workforce, they are expecting

peers and managers to communicate with them in a dynamic, two-way fashion

2. Technological change – as instant connectivity is the norm and social media platforms are growing more powerful, businesses are finding that traditional, one-way channels of communication are increasingly untenable

"Smart leaders today," say the authors, "engage with employees in a way that resembles ordinary person-to-person conversation more than it does a series of commands from on high."

Also contrast these conversations with conventional Performance Management processes. Here the focus is frequently on the system and the paperwork, rather than on the quality of the conversations and the relationship. We have long made a distinction between the *process* of performance management and the *spirit*. The process focuses on entering the data and holding the appraisal sessions on time. The spirit, so often lacking, should be a genuine, two-way conversation between manager and team member to understand what they have achieved, the strengths they have demonstrated, where their focus needs to be in the year ahead and the development they need and seek to grow and be fulfilled in their role and career.

In this book we will show you why conversations matter – how they are fundamental to the performance of your team and organisation, and how conversations create triggers in our brains related to our most basic instincts for survival. We will also show you how to integrate these five specific conversations into your daily life as a leader together with the changes of mindset and beliefs that will lead you to make a permanent emotional commitment to leading in this way. And at the end of this book you'll find some conversation toolkits – practical planners and checklists you can use to help you put the conversations into action.

Be brave and try them out. You will feel the power of building deeper and more trusting relationships at work.

CHAPTER 2

Why do conversations matter – the business case

Before looking at our five specific conversations, let's take some time to explore why conversations are so important.

In the previous chapter we proposed that conversations help build relationships which in turn promote employee engagement and have a critical impact on business performance. So what's the evidence – what links are there between employee engagement and business performance?

How can employee engagement be defined?

First of all, let's define employee engagement. There are a number of definitions, but the one we find most helpful describes employee engagement as having three key features:

- Employees having a sense of *organisational citizenship* – being proud to belong to their organisation, and being advocates of its products and services to other potential employees and customers

- Employees being willing to give their *discretionary effort* – to go the extra mile, or put in those additional hours when needed

- Employees having an *intention to stay* – coupled with a belief that they have room to grow and fulfil their potential and career aspirations within the organisation

Employee *engagement* is therefore different from the earlier measure of employee *satisfaction* that many organisations monitor. Employees may be satisfied at work with their role, terms and conditions or working conditions, but not necessarily willing to demonstrate whole-hearted commitment. Engagement on the other hand is exactly about their willingness to go above and beyond their standard job description because they believe in their organisation, are committed to serving their customers and proud to belong.

Why is employee engagement so important?

Before we come on to the evidence of the link between high levels of engagement and superior business performance it's worth touching on the possible reasons for this linkage. The most powerful is that employee engagement drives customer advocacy. Customer advocacy should arguably be the ultimate goal of all organisations – that state where customers are so positive about their experience of doing business with you that they proactively and consciously recommend you to other potential customers. And as the CEO of a Fortune 500 healthcare company told us,

"We can only achieve high levels of customer advocacy if our front line teams, the people our customers interact with every day, are themselves passionate about and committed to the services we provide."

Now let's look at the research

All the research points to the fact that the higher employee engagement is rated, the more successful the organisation – in sales, profit, return on investment and customer satisfaction. The evidence gathered by MacLeod and Clarke in their 2009 report "Engaging for Success" [5] showed clear, defined and repeated correlations between employee engagement and organisational success. More recently the Engage for Success workgroup's report "Nailing the Evidence" [6] also underscored these links, highlighting research evidence from Aon Hewitt [7], Gallup [8], Hay [9], Kenexa [10] and Towers Watson [11], amongst others, which year after year consistently demonstrate the benefits of high employee engagement across the full range of business performance metrics.

Key statistics from Nailing the Evidence [6]

REVENUE GROWTH

Organisations in the top quartile of engagement scores demonstrated **revenue growth** 2.5 times greater than those in the bottom quartile.

PROFIT

Companies with engagement scores in the top quartile had **twice the annual net profit** of those in the bottom quartile.

PRODUCTIVITY

Organisations in the top quartile of employee engagement scores had **18% higher productivity** than those in the bottom quartile.

INNOVATION

59% of engaged employees said that their job brings out their most **creative ideas** against 3% of those less engaged.

CUSTOMER SATISFACTION

Companies with top quartile engagement scores average **12% higher customer advocacy.**

EMPLOYEE TURNOVER

Companies with high levels of engagement show turnover rate **40% lower** than companies with low levels of engagement.

"Nailing the Evidence" concludes, "No wonder 94% of the world's most admired companies believe that their efforts to engage their employees have created a competitive advantage."

What do actual levels of employee engagement look like globally, and what is the potential impact of these levels of engagement for the countries concerned? In 2012 Kenexa [12] reported these percentages of engagement by country:

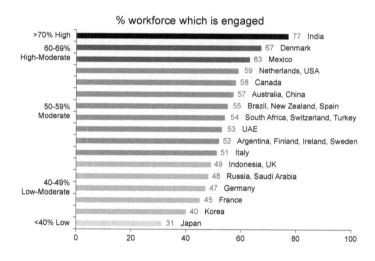

% workforce which is engaged

>70% High	77 India
60-69% High-Moderate	67 Denmark
	63 Mexico
	59 Netherlands, USA
	58 Canada
	57 Australia, China
50-59% Moderate	55 Brazil, New Zealand, Spain
	54 South Africa, Switzerland, Turkey
	53 UAE
	52 Argentina, Finland, Ireland, Sweden
	51 Italy
	49 Indonesia, UK
	48 Russia, Saudi Arabia
40-49% Low-Moderate	47 Germany
	45 France
	40 Korea
<40% Low	31 Japan

Why should these nations care about their low engagement scores? We go back to what Jim Clifton of Gallup says: "… there will be plenty of new potential customers in the coming decades. Right now, the world's GDP is US$60 trillion, and that figure will grow to US$200 trillion in the next 30 years. Simply put, the global economy will have US$140 trillion worth of new customers. When and if your company, and then country, doubles its workforce engagement, only great things will follow: an economic boom, an explosion of innovative ideas, and a surge in entrepreneurship. No country can ramp up ideas and entrepreneurship high enough right now. There are literally trillions in customer revenue waiting to be won." [3]

What drives high levels of employee engagement?

MacLeod and Clarke [5] identify the following four key factors:

1. Visible, empowering leadership that provides a strong strategic narrative about the organisation – where it has come from and where it is going

2. Engaging managers who:

   • Focus their people and give them scope to innovate and contribute

   • Treat their people as individuals – and build individual relationships

   • Coach and stretch their people

3. The voice of the employee is heard throughout the organisation – so that information and ideas do not just flow downwards from the top, but cascade upwards too

4. There is organisational integrity – where the values on the wall are reflected in day-to-day behaviours

They comment that, "These four factors emerge consistently, time after time, and in all geographies as the drivers of employee engagement."

And this brings us to the (maybe literally) sixty-four million dollar question. *What can organisations actually do, in down-to-earth, practical terms,* to influence these drivers of employee engagement in order to achieve employee engagement scores in the top quartile of comparable organisations?

You may have experienced first-hand some of the initiatives that organisations have adopted, which tend to include surveys and organisation-wide communications – but is it having a big enough impact?

The Head of Employee Engagement for a leading international energy company told us,

"I've been in this role for seven years. Each year we've run our Employee Engagement survey and been unhappy with the results. I create an action plan with roadshows and presentations. Everyone does their duty and participates, but nothing actually changes. This year I'm doing something different. I'm targeting first line managers and giving them training in how to build closer relationships with their people by holding engaging conversations."

Why are companies switching focus from organisation-wide actions to focusing on what individual managers can do?

This Head of Employee Engagement isn't alone. Increasingly companies are becoming frustrated at the lack of impact that their company-wide, top-down initiatives are having, and are looking at ways of improving engagement from the bottom up; manager by manager. We know from Gallup's research [3] that the primary driver of an employee's feelings of engagement is the quality of the relationship they feel they have with their immediate line manager. It is often said that we "join a company, but leave a manager" and the research shows this to be truer than we knew.

More and more organisations are therefore focusing directly on giving line managers the tools, skills and confidence to build closer and more trusting relationships with members of their teams.

How can you build trusting relationships?

As we will see in a later chapter, trust comes from a combination of factors, such as credibility, reliability and intimacy. But even if you understand those factors, how can you build them? With so many factors that can impact on trust, how can a manager know which factors are most important and where to place most effort?

There have been many research studies into the issues of trust. Atkinson and Butcher [13] propose that there are two main bases of trust in a managerial context:

- task-based competence: based on factors such as professional competence, reputation and role legitimacy

- personal motives: based on factors such as communication, social interaction and personality traits

They concluded that although 'utility' relationships – where the focus is on what the other person can provide – can function just on competence-based trust, 'personal' relationships – where the focus is on the relationship with the other person and giving it commitment and emotional attachment – requires high levels of both competence- and motive-based trust. They also found that personal relationships are perceived to be of higher value to the parties involved and bring more benefit than utility relationships.

There have even been investigations into the different factors which impact on trust. For example, in the Journal of Business Studies Quarterly, Shpëtim Çerri presented a statistical analysis of which factors have the greatest correlation with the quality of business relationships [14]. Çerri took the five factors that are most commonly cited in academic research as having an impact on trust, as well as testing out the hypothesis that trust is positively correlated with relationship quality. The diagram below shows his findings in terms of the order in which the factors impact on trust, with social interactions having the greatest correlation and personality traits the least.

Factors which impact on trust in order of strength of correlation

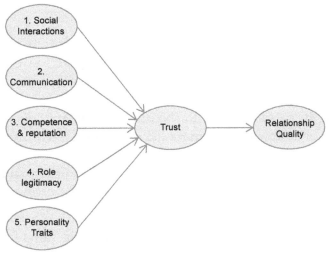

From Shpëtim Çerri, Journal of Business Studies Quarterly, 2012, Vol. 4

Çerri's results echo research from a wide number of industries. When it comes down to it, a manager's ability to have meaningful social interactions and communications has the most impact on the trust within a relationship.

And as we have seen, at the heart of this is the ability and emotional commitment to hold authentic, open, two-way human conversations. As Groysberg & Slind observe:

"Today's leaders achieve far more engagement and credibility when they take part in genuine conversation with the people who work for and with them." [4]

Conversations that aim to **build trusting relationships** between you and your team members help you to build strong individual relationships with each member of your team, a key driver of engagement. They also contribute to organisational integrity, where there is synergy between the values you promote and the behaviour you demonstrate.

Conversations about **mutual expectations** and the "why" you are seeking to achieve certain goals help to give your people that vital sense of strategic narrative – where the organisation is going and why it matters. These conversations also help people to feel stretched and developed.

Conversations that show **genuine appreciation** can help to give people even more scope to innovate and contribute from their own unique skill set.

Conversations that **challenge unhelpful behaviour** are also key to organisational integrity as behaviour that is inconsistent with espoused values can be challenged and modified.

Finally, conversations that seek to **build the future** together make a major contribution to people feeling coached and developed – and having a genuine career path that contributes to an intention to stay.

In summary

So in summary, there is a chain reaction:

The chain reaction from conversations through to business performance

Employee engagement has moved to the mainstream of business concern, and become a key metric for all the world's leading organisations. After reading this chapter you can understand why. But what often fails to be addressed is what organisations can actually do in practical terms to improve it.

Here, for the first time, we offer a practical approach that focuses on giving insights into the conversations you can hold that will improve the quality of the relationships you have with members of your team. And as a result you will have a profound, positive impact on their feelings of engagement.

CHAPTER 3

Why do conversations matter
– the neuroscience case

Having looked at the importance of conversations in improving business performance, in this chapter we review the latest neuroscience insights on why relationships matter, and how leaders can modify their behaviour to build trust and engagement. In particular we see what neuroscience tells us about the physical impact of conversations, and how those insights can help us prepare for the conversations we need to have.

What is neuroscience?

Neuroscience is an exploding field of research, driven by new techniques such as MRI (magnetic resonance imaging) which allow scientists to see changes within the brain as people feel different emotions, make decisions or deal with problems. There are powerful insights from this research which can help leaders to become more conscious of the impact of their behaviour, moods and emotions on others, and to modify them in order to build trust, relationships and collaboration.

These insights start with a simple proposition called the triune brain hypothesis (originally developed by Paul D MacLean in 1970 and developed further in his work "The Triune Brain in Evolution" in 1990 [15]) which helps us to understand the role that different parts of the brain play in dealing with threats, rewards and relationships. In this theory the brain is said to be made up of three overlapping elements – the brain stem (or reptile brain), the mammalian (or limbic brain) and the human (or thinking brain). Because evolution cannot "un-make" what our DNA is programmed to build in each new human being, it has to build new features on top of those that are already in place. So whether we like it or not, our human brains contain these three components and they all have the potential to drive our behaviour – either consciously or unconsciously.

The three parts of the brain

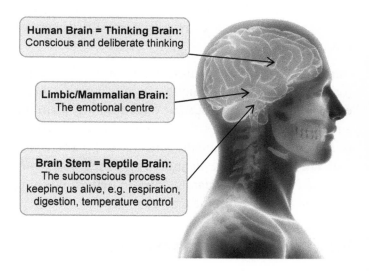

Human Brain = Thinking Brain:
Conscious and deliberate thinking

Limbic/Mammalian Brain:
The emotional centre

Brain Stem = Reptile Brain:
The subconscious process
keeping us alive, e.g. respiration,
digestion, temperature control

The job of our reptile brain is to pursue survival. Located at the top of the spine it regulates hundreds of vital activities such as breathing, heart rate, liver function, waking and sleeping – in fact everything that is unconscious and life-critical. And it is just as well that it does so, as we would be totally overloaded with data and decision-making if we had to manage these things with our conscious brain.

On top of our reptile brain sits our mammalian brain which evolved when mammals first appeared, bearing live young and needing to nurture and care for them. This is where emotions, feelings and relationships are shaped and managed, and where some of the most powerful drivers of our behaviour are located – even though we might not realise it. Typically human beings are said to have seven basic emotions: anger, disgust, fear, sadness, happiness and love plus surprise or "startle" which mediates the strength of the other emotions. The first four are often called negative emotions but are still extremely powerful drivers of our behaviour.

Finally, on top of the mammalian brain sits the human (or thinking) brain. Unique to humans this brain enables us to do conscious, rational thinking, planning and acting. And here's the problem. Our *ability* to think, plan and act rationally misleads us into believing that rational thinking, planning and acting is *actually what drives our behaviour* as human beings. Nothing could be further from the truth.

What drives our behaviour?

What we now understand is that much of our behaviour is driven by our emotional mammalian brains, and our thinking brain then rationalises this behaviour so that we convince ourselves that what we have said or done is rational and logical. In fact we can all recognise that a decision to spend money on a new car, or phone or fashion accessory is driven by how it feels, and then later we find rational arguments to justify our purchase to ourselves or our partner. Equally, this is what is happening when we make an instant decision about a candidate at the start of a selection interview (based on an emotional "gut reaction"), and then spend the rest of the interview searching for data to back up our initial decision.

What is less well appreciated is that, as Steven Pinker the cognitive scientist puts it, "our most ardent emotions are evoked... by other people" [16]. Unconsciously we are continuously monitoring how we feel about the people around us – at work and outside work. In situations of collaboration, or trade, or potential conflict we are asking ourselves "How far can I trust this person?" We search unconsciously for those miniscule changes in facial expression or language tone that give us the confidence to trust, or make us wary, cautious and suspicious. Evolution has programmed us to be expert human lie detectors.

In the past it was believed that the complexity of the human brain evolved as a result of the opportunities for evolutionary advantage provided by the use of ever more complex and sophisticated tools. Many scientists now believe that far and away the most complex activity our brain manages, and which drives its incredible complexity, is the management of our relationships with other people. In other words, *the brain is the "organ of relationship"*. Some scientists describe homo sapiens as a "hyper-social" species, to make the same point. Yet because we are largely unconscious of the immense skill, dexterity and speed with which we use language, gesture, facial expression, mood and emotion to manage our relationships with those around us, we vastly underestimate the complexity of the process.

What else causes us to be emotional rather than rational?

It is worth mentioning one further component of the brain that can also explain our sometimes "irrational" behaviour – the amygdala. Located deep in the brain, near the limbic system, the amygdala performs primary roles in the formation and storage of memories associated with emotional events. These memories then provide us with a fundamental system which causes us to *move towards* people, events or situations that will provide rewards and pleasure, and *away from* people or situations we associate with risk and threat.

It is the amygdala that sets off the flight or fight reaction we are all so familiar with: the racing heart and other physiological changes that get us ready for urgent action.

Not only is the amygdala designed to withdraw oxygen from the thinking brain – so you are more likely to act on your impulses – but more interestingly the kind of thought processes that you have in your head become repetitive. In the workplace it can sound like 'I will look foolish; people will dislike me; there will be an argument ...' looping round in your head, so all you're getting is a heightened state of fear which is having a huge impact on your senses and muscles.

And of course the amygdala's instantaneous response to the possibility of a threat makes complete sense in evolutionary terms. If the sound of a twig snapping behind you in the forest startles you, setting off the fight or flight response, and scaring others around you with your reaction, that's a good thing for your survival. If there really is no threat, you were scared but you survived. It there was a real threat you were ready to react to it, and optimised your chances of surviving.

The phrase "amygdala hijack" was a term coined by Daniel Goleman in his book *Emotional Intelligence* [17.] He uses the term to describe extreme emotional reactions from people which come out before their rational mind can regulate their behaviour. We've all had the experience of doing something in the heat of the moment and then regretting it later. So why does this happen?

When faced with a situation which is threatening, the stimulus goes immediately to the thalamus, the part of the brain which relays motor and sensory signals to other parts of the brain, which decide how to respond. It sends signals to both the amygdala and to the neocortex (the "thinking brain"). Realising that this is a fight or flight situation, the amygdala sends a rush of stress hormones through the body, hijacking the thinking brain, which – as it reacts slightly more slowly than the amygdala – doesn't have a chance to regulate the reaction. This can lead the person to react irrationally and potentially destructively.

We feel fear at the prospect of a difficult conversation or presentation to five hundred people because our brain has not evolved for success in the modern world, but for success as hunter-gatherers on the plains of Africa. Sophisticated hominids are only one or two million years old, we have probably only had complex language for 40,000 years and we have only had agriculture and lived in cities for 10,000 years. We are evolved for success in small groups of related individuals on the savannah where safety came from vigilance against predators and threats from rival groups and from trusting collaboration within the group.

So the problem is that our brains don't recognise the difference between a difficult conversation and a sabre-toothed tiger!

What are the implications of these insights for leaders seeking to build trusting relationships with those who work for and with them?

We take three key lessons:

First, that leaders need to avoid (consciously or unconsciously) demonstrating behaviour that people's primitive brains will perceive as creating threats, risks or danger. When this happens we know that deep-seated responses kick in that cause people to be closed, defensive and suspicious.

Second, that leaders need to be aware of the importance of creating conditions that will not only appeal to people's rational brains, but also their positive emotions creating a *towards* reaction, and a key way to do this is through authentic, honest, two-way conversations.

And third – that you can't fake it. Other people are too good at detecting insincerity. You need to look within yourself, put your own ego and needs to one side, and seek to genuinely understand and relate to the other person. This is not about being soft, but it is about honestly seeking a meaningful, high-quality relationship.

How can you use these insights in practical ways to build relationships?

We use a useful mnemonic, FIVEC, to help us understand various factors in a relationship which can build trust. The more these factors are present, the more likely they will encourage positive emotions from the other person and create a *towards* reaction to us. When these aspects aren't present, or their opposite is, then they pose a risk or threat to the other person which will drive them away from us.

The FIVEC factors which affect trust in a relationship

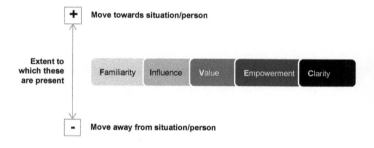

Familiarity: Familiarity or intimacy refers to the feeling of being in a close personal association with another person. Familiarity in human relationships requires dialogue, transparency, vulnerability, and reciprocity. Traditionally leaders have been taught that building familiarity with those who work for them is an undesirable characteristic – even dangerous and likely to undermine their authority as leaders. New leaders are often taught to keep their distance from their teams. We now know that creating opportunities and investing time to deeply understand members of your team, and to be prepared to reveal something of yourself, pays off in minimising their perception of you as a threat or rival, and builds loyalty by appealing to people's need to belong and to feel appreciated for who they are. Becoming more familiar with a person helps us develop the level of mutual trust we feel with them and, as this increases, we feel more comfortable and willing to discuss and share critical information. Perhaps we should re-state the old saying as "familiarity breeds contentment".

Influence: The level of influence you have over another individual has an impact on the perceived threat you can indirectly or directly create in them and vice versa. Influence at work is often related to positional power and the associated status symbols such as bigger desks, better offices or a different uniform or dress code. If you are the manager, your level of influence over your team member will be greater than the influence you have over your own manager. Other types of influence that can impact the *away from* and *towards* responses include interpersonal or social influence, resource control, technical expertise and other socio-economic factors by which we judge relative status.

Value: People need to feel valued and respected for who they are and what they do. They also have a deep need to feel they are being treated with fairness. When people feel valued it generates a *towards* response, and when not valued, an *away from* response. People can't know that you value them and their contribution unless you talk to them and tell them about it. How often have we heard leaders at work say, "Why should I say thank you to him / her? They are just doing the job they are being paid for." Well, now we know that people are not mindless automatons, but deeply driven by the emotions they feel from how they are treated, and the satisfaction they get from what they do at work. Taking the time to understand the contribution a team member is making, and authentically telling them how much you value that contribution, is a key part of building a long-term trusting relationship, and thus their engagement to go the extra mile.

Empowerment: Empowerment refers to the degree of freedom to act that people feel they have in their daily work. Numerous studies show that in today's world of work where people are contributing their creativity and imagination to the organisation, a feeling of empowerment is vital in building engagement and commitment. Conversely, being micro-managed or controlled is seen as a threat. But remember that the level of freedom and autonomy people need to thrive and generate a *towards* response varies from person to person and differs at different stages of their personal and career development. Too much empowerment at too early a stage, or too little empowerment too late, could generate an *away from* response. It's therefore important to discuss what and where the boundaries are, and ensure the appropriate level of support, so that they – and the business – can thrive.

Clarity: Lack of clarity about the future is generally perceived as a threat, generating an *away from* response. Remember that our primitive brain is wondering where the next meal is coming from. However, it is impossible to provide clarity and certainty about the future all the time. As a leader what you can do at work is to recognise that people need and value clarity, and provide as much information as possible – even if that's saying nothing has changed.

The power of conversation in times of stress

A final insight into how an understanding of the brain can help leaders build more trusting relationships at work concerns the nature of "stress". Research into the stress hormone cortisol and the chemical oxytocin (which is linked to love, trust and attachment) shows that exposure to the voice of a loved (trusted) person reduces cortisol and increases oxytocin. The result is less stress and "feeling better".

In looking at the implications for leadership of neuroscience [18], experts Paul Brown and Brenda Hales highlight an article in the *Financial Times* magazine where Gillian Tett "featured the work of Professor Andrew Lo at MIT. Under the headline 'Periods of acute stress in the markets offer intriguing examples of how our brains work', she observed that when markets go into free-fall and traders are hugely stressed they abandon their computers as sources of information in favour of personal and telephone contact with people they know and trust… This spontaneous and non-conscious action to get stress hormone levels down and feel engaged by stimulating oxytocin makes us focus on how leaders need to 'humanise', or should we say 'brainwise' the workplace."

In summary

These latest insights from neuroscience help us to understand why open, two-way human conversations contribute towards building trust. They also give us powerful pointers as to the behaviour we can deliberately adopt and avoid to create a positive, constructive atmosphere in the conversations themselves.

CHAPTER 4

Getting ready to hold the conversations

Having discussed why relationships matter at work, and how insights from neuroscience can help us modify our behaviour to create a *towards* response, let's briefly look at the mindsets, feelings and beliefs that will help you to hold these conversations effectively. We've provided conversation planners at the back of this book to take you through the process of each conversation, but you'll never get to the point of planning the process of a conversation unless you've also taken into account your mindset, feelings and beliefs!

As discussed earlier, you don't need to be an expert conversationalist, talkative extrovert or a self-confident influencer in order for the conversations to work. In fact it probably helps if you are none of these!

What's much more important is your *intention* and *beliefs.*

Intention is about the motives that are in your heart as you start to try out the conversations with your colleagues and team members. Recall from the chapter on neuroscience that we are all expert lie detectors. We do this unconsciously and we do it not just by listening to the words and questions but also by unconsciously sensing the underlying motives of our colleague through their eye contact, expressions, voice tone, mood and body language. As a result we intuitively feel whether their interest in us is genuine and authentic, or fake and self-serving.

Beliefs refers to the idea that much of our behaviour is driven by, often unconscious, beliefs that we hold about ourselves or others that can be either enabling or limiting. If you hold a belief that "relationships at work don't matter", albeit unconsciously, this may be a limiting belief that gets in the way of you investing effort to build strong relationships at work and will drive your behaviour accordingly. If you can identify this belief, challenge it and re-frame it as an enabling belief, this can be a powerful driver of new and different behaviour, for example, "Positive relationships with key colleagues will help me to be more effective at work, and to enjoy my work more."

Of course it helps to prepare thoroughly, to think about the questions and comments you will use in the conversation, and to pay attention to things like eye contact and body language. But it's just as important to spend a few moments to reflect honestly on your intention and beliefs in holding each conversation. Here are some questions to ask yourself as you embark on this journey.

Will

How well do you really *want* to know the members of your team? Start with the basics. How long have they been in their role? What did they do before? What are their interests and passions outside work? What are the names of their partner and children? What are they doing in their lives? If you don't know the answers to these basic questions, do you really *want* to go deeper? Or does it make you feel uncomfortable that you can't answer some of these questions? It's not too late. If you have the *will* to start building deeper and more trusting relationships, you *can* do it.

Legacy

How do you want to be remembered as a leader? What stories do you want people to tell about you when you have moved on to your next role? What stories will people actually tell about you? What footprint will you have left? When confronted with these questions leaders often start with lists of *what* they will have achieved, then on deeper reflection ask themselves about *how* they will have achieved it. Will people remember the trust they had in you, your care and humanity, the atmosphere of fun and achievement that you created for the team, the opportunities for development you afforded them?

Relationships

How much do the quality of your relationships at work (and outside) matter to you? When they stop to reflect on this question, many leaders conclude that the quality of the relationships they have in their lives is actually the most important thing of all. The *quality of the connections* we have with others not only gets things done but defines the sense of fulfilment and pleasure we get from our work.

Courage

Why do these conversations so rarely happen at work? In the following chapters we offer some of the reasons related to us by participants in 5 Conversations workshops. But there's always one deeper, underlying reason. Holding these conversations *takes courage.* As we try them out and gradually find that our fears are unfounded, we become more willing to hold them. They feel like less of a risk. But in prospect, if you have not been used to deeply questioning and listening to others, nor being vulnerable and open about yourself, they do seem like a risk. What will you learn? What might you reveal? What will people think about you? How will the conversations affect your reputation? Will you find yourself in difficult situations, or knowing things about your people that you would rather not know?

Stewardship

How much do you really care about, not just the performance, but also the well-being of your team members? How strong is the *sense of stewardship* that guides your dealings with them? Is the quality of their working life important to you? How much do you want to see them succeed, thrive, flourish at work? Does it matter to you if they don't feel they are learning, developing, being stretched within your team? Does helping someone fulfil their potential and build their career give you a sense of fulfilment and deep satisfaction?

Curiosity

How good a listener are you? How good do you want to be? How can you learn to be even better? What mindset can you adopt that will enable you to be deeply curious about the *hopes, dreams and fears* of members of your team and other colleagues with whom you work? How will you feel when you have more deeply understood the aspirations and drivers of all those who surround you at work?

Mindfulness

A final element of preparation is captured by the idea of "mindfulness". With its roots in Buddhism, the meditation techniques involved in mindfulness – with its principles of attentiveness to the present and observing without criticising – have gained popularity worldwide as a method to handle emotions. In the context of preparing to hold a conversation it means taking a few quiet minutes to achieve a state of calmness and relaxation in which you turn down the dial on the chatter of self-talk that fills your head every minute. It means focusing clearly on the needs of the other person and resolving to listen attentively to them with your whole self. And then in the conversation itself mindfulness means bringing your complete attention to the present experience on a moment-to-moment basis, being conscious of what is happening without judging it, and being "present" for your colleague. Can you clear your mind and approach the conversation in an attentive and non-judgemental way, or is your mind too distracted and your thinking too clouded by previous prejudices to make the conversation effective?

Are you ready?

We hope that reflecting on the ideas and questions above help you to be fully prepared to hold a great conversation with your colleague and make it more likely that you will summon the bravery to start holding these conversations. And then, when you have felt their power, you will add them into your daily working life as a natural part of what you do, why you do it and who you are.

CHAPTER 5

Conversation 1
Establishing a trusting
relationship

A colleague describes this experience early in his career:

Twenty-five years ago I had just launched my one man consultancy business as a provider of recruitment and assessment services to large IT companies. I had just won my first client through a long-standing relationship with the HR VP who had been my boss in a previous life. The client was a large IT business and I was to provide a selection and recruitment service to the Sales & Marketing function, based in London. A couple of weeks into the assignment I was scheduled to meet with the VP for Sales & Marketing. This was a critical meeting as he needed to approve the decision of the HR VP to hire me, and I needed to gain his confidence that I could provide the services his function needed. This would have been enough to make me nervous anyway, but my unease at the prospect of meeting him was increased by the reputation he had gained since joining the company a few months earlier – as a tough, ruthless operator who didn't suffer fools.

The day arrived when I was scheduled to meet him, having spent the previous evening preparing my pitch. I genuinely had no idea how the meeting would go, but I was certain that I would have to answer tough and searching questions about my experience, credentials and recommendations for how I would complete the assignment for his part of the business.

At the appointed hour I was seated in the reception area outside his office, trying to relax whilst I waited to be called into his office. Finally the moment arrived and I heard his voice over the intercom asking his PA to show me in to his office. I gathered my papers and stepped inside as she opened the door and ushered me in.

To my surprise he rose from behind his desk and strode over, extending his hand, and shook mine with a warm smile and greeting. He invited me to sit in some casual chairs alongside a coffee table where he also sat. Tea and coffee were nearby and he filled a mug for me. He then turned to me and said, "So, John, tell me all about yourself and your business."

Taken aback at his warmth I stumbled through my background and my plans and dreams for my little company. Throughout he smiled and nodded, keeping eye contact and showing real interest in me and my plans. Within a few minutes I relaxed, beginning to enjoy the opportunity to talk about myself and my company. For 45 minutes he gave me his undivided attention and showed genuine curiosity in me. I felt completely at ease and energised by his interest in me.

In the last 15 minutes he told me about the selection and assessment challenges his function was facing, and the support that he needed from me over the next few months.

I left his office feeling motivated and 100% committed to doing the best possible job I could for him in the months ahead, and I did indeed go way beyond the call of duty to meet his needs and deliver a great service for him over this period and then several years beyond.

Looking back I could be cynical and say that he was using his obvious skills as a super sales person to win my commitment. But in a way that doesn't matter. The point is that I believed and felt that he was genuinely interested in me and my little business, and that had a massive impact on my commitment to go the extra mile for him. And because his warmth was so unexpected, the impact was doubly powerful.

What this conversation is about

Think about the people you work with. There will be the boss you work for; there will be the people who work for you; there will be your peers, customers, suppliers and a whole range of other stakeholders inside your organisation and outside. Now think about the quality of the relationships you have with some of these people. Some will be easy, natural, open and positive. Others may be shallow, strained or even downright difficult.

This conversation is about taking conscious steps to establish a deeper and more trusting relationship with key members of your team, and also with other key colleagues and stakeholders.

It's about creating a space to better understand and know each other in terms of who you are, what you do, how you do it and why you do it. It's about listening to and sharing insights, stories and points of view about how you each see your role and the world around you. It's about having the intention and the courage to talk with each other about who you really are, and what matters to and drives each of you – and to be genuinely interested in and curious about the other person. It's about understanding each other's drivers, motivations and preferences. What gets you out of bed in the morning? What does a great day at work look like? When you are at the top of your game, what conditions are in place to cause this? What de-motivates you at work? It's about sharing this information with an open and non-judgemental frame of mind.

This conversation is about building trust – either when first getting to know each other as new colleagues at work, or when there is a benefit from re-building or deepening a relationship with a long-standing colleague. Trust is both a fuel into, and an output from, these conversations. The better the quality of the conversation the more trust develops – and the more that trust develops the better the quality of the conversation.

The trust pyramid illustrates how, as levels of trust increase, we are able to discuss deeper and more personal areas:

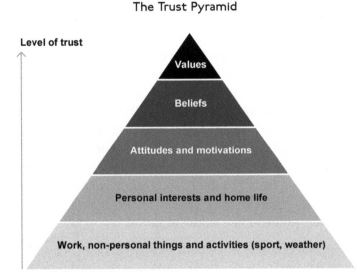

The Trust Pyramid

Level of trust

Values

Beliefs

Attitudes and motivations

Personal interests and home life

Work, non-personal things and activities (sport, weather)

Why this conversation matters

This conversation matters because as a leader, having trusting relationships with the people who work for you and with you is at the heart of getting things done. When trust exists in a relationship we are open to ideas, possibilities and collaboration. Where trust is absent we are closed, defensive and suspicious. Where a trusting relationship exists, we are likely to be engaged – proud to belong to our organisation, willing to go the extra mile and committed to building our career here. Trust improves efficiency by increasing the speed with which we work, and reducing bureaucracy and cost.

This conversation also enables you to tailor the way you work with each team member. It gives you the insights you need to fine-tune the way you delegate, coach, challenge and support them – to create the exact conditions they need to be engaged and deliver peak performance. Equally it enables your team member to understand how you work best and therefore modify their style to one in which you will both be successful and productive. And if this conversation doesn't happen early in your relationship with a new team member (either when they are new to your team, or you join as a new leader), you risk losing a vital opportunity to lay the foundations for the trusting relationship that is so vital to creating a high performing team and getting things done.

In the workplace trust is built through how we treat and interact with each other. The quality of conversations we have with each other matters deeply, but so does our behaviour in following up and acting consistently, honestly and congruently. A great conversation followed by unreliable or dishonest behaviour damages or destroys trust. The trust equation [19] powerfully captures this idea.

Trust Equation

$$\text{Trust} = \frac{\textbf{Credibility} + \textbf{Reliability} + \textbf{Intimacy}}{\textbf{Self Orientation}}$$

David H. Maister, Charles H. Green, Robert M. Galford: The Trusted Advisor, 2000

The trust equation suggests that the degree to which we are trusted by others is a function of four factors, three of which contribute positively towards how well we are trusted, and one negatively.

The three positive factors are our credibility, our reliability and the sense of intimacy the other person feels they have with us. Credibility is about our perceived competence and expertise, and the believability of our views and statements. Reliability is about both the degree to which we deliver what we promise, and also the predictability of our moods and emotions. Finally intimacy describes the closeness of the relationship people feel that they have with us. In the equation these three factors add to each other to make our trustworthiness positive.

However, the extent of our trustworthiness is then divided by the degree to which others perceive us to be self-orientated. In other words, if our in-built human lie detector picks up that we are actually in this primarily for selfish motives, to further our own ends, this dramatically reduces the degree to which others will trust us, despite any credibility, reliability or sense of intimacy we generate.

This conversation can make a positive contribution to all elements of the equation, but it has a special power in deepening intimacy and, when held with an authentic intention to build trust and understand our colleague, in reducing perceptions of self-orientation. This conversation also matters because we tend to fall into habits with our relationships – at work but also outside work. In marriage counselling it is common for counsellors to ask couples, "How much investment have you made in maintaining and building your relationship over the past few years?" Frequently couples are taken aback by the question. Over the years they have stopped being interested and curious about each other, letting their relationship get stuck on a plateau, or worse, allowing it to decline in small, undetectable steps as new experiences, feelings or values were not discussed and shared.

Similarly at work we often make the effort in a *new* relationship to establish some common ground – shared interests, people we know in common, similar career experiences – but after that we switch to auto-pilot and never think to try to take things deeper or even keep up to date. And of course with some relationships at work, perhaps that's fine. We can't have deep, meaningful, trusting relationships with everyone. But at other times it does matter, especially when you are a leader seeking to build a team to deliver challenging, stretching organisational objectives in times of change and stress.

A colleague was working with the top 60 partners of a global law firm at their international conference in Singapore. The theme of the event was "Building Trust and Collaboration" so the partners had been asked to practise holding this conversation with a colleague from another part of the world whom they knew less well. After the practice session, she was facilitating a discussion about the impact and usefulness of the conversation and one participant made a fascinating point:

"I would often have this conversation during a selection interview, to find out what makes the candidate tick. It never crossed my mind that you could have this same conversation after they had joined!"

If you make the time to initiate and hold this conversation with an open, honest intent, you make it more likely that people you rely on will be prepared to go the extra mile for you in the moments when it really matters. Conversely, if you neglect these conversations, take people for granted and rely upon a purely transactional relationship, you risk a transactional response from others in those moments when achievement of important goals hangs in the balance.

Finally, this conversation can provide a foundation for all your subsequent conversations. Having started this conversation, or held this as the first in a series of conversations to better understand each other, it becomes easier and more comfortable to initiate the next conversation, whether that's about sharing mutual expectations or challenging unhelpful behaviour.

Why this conversation often does not happen at work

For many leaders this conversation is simply not on their radar. Their work life is full of tasks, activities, deliverables, decisions and deadlines. Their interactions with their team members are purely transactional, made up of instructions, demands and requests. And the more the pressure builds, the greater the intensity of these transactional interactions. But for most of us, even a small opportunity for reflection is enough for the realisation to dawn that we have been neglecting the quality of our relationships with team members and others, and that there will be immeasurable benefit in terms of *team and business performance* from re-booting these relationships.

Another reason this conversation doesn't happen is the (sometimes unspoken) belief that it's dangerous for a leader's authority for them to become too close to their people; people need to respect their leaders and if they become too close, or worse appear to be trying to ingratiate themselves with members of their team, people will take advantage by slacking at work or bending the rules.

Let's deal with this objection head on. Firstly, we are not recommending or suggesting that the purpose of this conversation is to become friends with members of your team or have a relationship with them outside work. Instead we are talking about a trusting work relationship of mutual respect and shared understanding of what motivates and drives you both at work.

Secondly, we now have a much deeper understanding of what motivates people at work today, and being in awe of a distant authority figure doesn't feature in the mix. Perhaps there was a time in the last hundred years of business life when a leader in an organisation could use their authority to get things done through control, threats or bribes (though we doubt this ever resulted in genuine engagement and commitment). But many thinkers, from Abraham Maslow and Douglas McGregor to Frederick Herzberg and most recently Daniel Pink in *Drive* [20], have shown that real motivation must come from within. Pink shows that in today's world where you need people to bring their creative intelligence to work, we are really driven by our needs for autonomy, purpose and mastery. If your role as a leader is to create conditions in which your people can achieve these conditions, then this conversation is an essential first stage in doing so. Keeping your distance to enhance your position of authority simply won't cut it.

Another reason this conversation does not happen can be the feeling of vulnerability it can cause in you. How much will you feel comfortable revealing about yourself to a colleague? What if they ask you questions about yourself that you can't or don't want to answer? We now know that revealing vulnerability can be one of the most powerful ways of building trust, but the prospect may still leave you feeling uneasy. Our answer is that in the conversation you *do* have control over how much you reveal about yourself, and you need to trust your judgement in the moment as to how far to go. The more trust you build with your colleague, the further up the trust pyramid you can go with a feeling of security.

And now that you are thinking about having this conversation with someone at work, you may encounter another, internal barrier to holding it, especially with colleagues you have worked with for some time. You may be feeling awkward about revealing to them that you don't know as much about them as they would expect you to. Because of this, how will they react? What will they think of you? What will you reveal about yourself? Our response would be – be brave! Chances are your colleague will welcome and embrace the opportunity you are creating.

One of our colleagues works almost exclusively with start-ups and SMEs, especially in innovative technical fields, and chairs a small charity. She reports, "Since becoming aware of the 5 conversations, I've used them with organisations with as few as ten people. In fact I find where the teams are small, relationship issues appear to be much bigger and have potentially catastrophic effects. Smaller businesses have the same problems hiring and firing as everyone else, but the impacts and costs are relatively greater. In the charity I work with, I used the 'building a trusting relationship' conversation with one manager that the Board viewed as difficult and was immediately overwhelmed with the positive impact it had on that person as she expressed her relief. I simply asked her, 'Would you like to work with me on building a more trusting relationship?' It had an immense impact on me too."

Finally, it's worth saying that we are not idealistic about how this conversation will turn out each time you hold it – and nor do we advocate that you should be. It's inevitable that sometimes you will make a close and warm connection with your colleague quickly, and at other times that connection will be harder to establish. But even if you just make a small step forward in building the relationship, chances are you will feel this is worthwhile and resolve to come back and build on this in a future conversation.

Why this conversation works

This conversation works because it appeals in particular to two of the five key factors that drive our *towards* or *away from* behaviours – familiarity and value. Recall that familiarity means having a shared sense of intimacy with another person. A conversation to share your needs, drivers, feelings and preferences with another human being, in which you are listened to and appreciated, cannot help but deepen the sense of familiarity and intimacy you have with that person. And the fact that another person has taken the time to give you their full and undivided attention, and shared with you their own needs and drivers, cannot help but make you feel valued.

And of course you don't need to agree with each other on every point in order to develop familiarity and feel valued. Often understanding each other better but acknowledging how you are different will have the same effect. **The great thing about this conversation is that it provides a platform for the relationship to be maintained and extended over time by providing insights, reference points and mutual interests that can be renewed and built upon.**

A colleague, Catalina, was coaching Luis, a senior client who managed a team of seven people in a venture capital company. One of Luis's concerns was that he felt that his team didn't particularly like him. As he worked in the same office as his team, Catalina asked him to draw a diagram of the office and show where everyone sat, including himself. Luis drew the desks and put each person's name next to it. Then she asked him a series of questions:

"Who's got children?"

"Who has coffee in the morning and who has tea?"

"Who's the next person in the office to have a birthday?"

"Where are they going on holiday?"

Luis was stunned. He didn't know the answer to any of those questions. By contrast, he could tell her which clients each of his team managed, how much revenue they were bringing in and where they were in relation to their targets.

So why didn't he know the answers to those questions? Catalina asked him to describe what happened every day at the office. He would come into the office first thing, go straight to his desk and get working, and wouldn't really talk as he had so much to do (as did everyone else). He tended to do all his communications via email, including sending emails to people who were sitting only a few metres away from him, and his emails were all to do with work.

Having described this, Luis looked thoughtful.

The next time Catalina saw him he proudly brandished a spreadsheet: "I've got the answers to all of your questions!" And there it was, a spreadsheet containing the names of each of his team members and their children, drink preferences, birthdays, holidays and more!

An extreme thing to do, but what was going on? Several months after the coaching ended, Luis contacted Catalina and said how much difference her questions had made. OK, so he'd noted the answers down on a spreadsheet which may appear mechanistic, but the process he'd gone through to get those answers meant that now he was actually talking to his team, showing an interest in them, and getting to know them as a whole person and not just as an employee. And they were responding positively to his interest and their performance was getting even better! He added that this had also helped him with his clients. He'd always found it difficult to have small talk, but now that he understands that small talk helps to build a relationship which will then make clients more likely to want to do business with him, he no longer avoids it.

The practicalities of holding this conversation

A. Identifying *who* to have the conversation with, and *why* and *when* it will be helpful

Think about and note down the people in your team where there is potential benefit from deepening your relationship. (Of course you can think about colleagues and other stakeholders outside your team where this conversation may also be very useful.) Some obvious situations would include:

- A new or recently joined member of your team – and of course this is a great conversation to have on the first or second day that they join your team, perhaps building on discussions you had during the selection process

- You have just joined as a new leader of the team and need to build relationships quickly with each member of your new team

- You realise that, although you have worked together for some time with a team member or colleague, your relationship is quite transactional, you don't really know each other deeply, *and* there would be some business or operational benefit from understanding each other better and building a more trusting relationship

- You are in an existing or newly formed team which is about to face some difficult challenges or change

- You need to build a deeper and more trusting relationship with your boss

In summary, it is never too late to have this conversation – and it is never too early!

B. Setting up the conversation and issuing an invitation to it

Every situation is unique, and each of us has our own preferred ways of working and communicating, but in all cases we recommend these three simple steps:

1. Write down the name of the person you plan to have the conversation with, together with *why* building a deeper and more trusting relationship with them will benefit you both *and* the business.

"I need to have this conversation with Mary. She is a new sales executive in my team. If I can build a trusting relationship quickly, and better understand her strengths and preferred ways of working, I will be able to better match sales accounts to her, and give her the coaching she needs to be successful. If she can get to know my values and what matters to me, that will give her the best chance of being successful quickly. And being successful will benefit her financially, and will help deliver the results we need in the team and for the business."

2. Use the words above to frame an invitation – being conscious of how elements of the FIVEC model can accidentally cause an away reaction – and invite a response.

"Hi Mary – I would find it really useful if we could make some time to get to know each other better and share our values and preferred ways of working. That will help me work out the best accounts to match to your strengths, and how best to support you in being successful in your first few months in the team. How does that sound to you? Shall we agree a date and an agenda?"

3. Prepare yourself to be at your best in the conversation, using the following steps:

   a. Head: Am I really clear about why holding this conversation will benefit me, my colleague and the business?

   b. Hand: Have I thought through, and planned, the agenda and questions that will be most helpful in making this conversation go well?

   c. Heart: Have I examined my intentions and motivations in holding this conversation, and ensured that there is no element of "self-orientation" in my heart? Have I reminded myself that this conversation is not about me but is driven by a genuine curiosity to understand my colleague better, and develop a more trusting relationship? Am I prepared to be open and reveal something about myself?

C. Planning the agenda for the conversation

Plan the agenda for the conversation, especially the questions you will ask and invite. We recommend using the following question to open the conversation:

"What would you most like to ask me that will help you to understand me better?"

Allow time for your response and for the conversation to develop. Volunteer additional information they may not have asked about.

Now turn it around and invite them to tell you about themselves.

Questions both of you could consider to continue and open up the conversation include:

- Questions which reveal what they value, for example: "What's really important to you at work?" "What do you feel most strongly about?" "What are you most passionate about?"

- Questions which indicate how they view themselves, for example: "What do you consider your greatest strength?" "What are you most proud of?" "What do you think is your greatest limitation?" "What do you want to be known for?" "What is it that you really stand for?"

- Questions which show what's important to them in their relationships with others, for example: "What's important to you in building a relationship with someone?" "What matters most to you when trusting others?" "When do you tend to feel most badly let down by a colleague?" "What sorts of things destroy a relationship for you?" "To what extent do you tend to open up to others at work?" "How easily do you trust others?" "What one thing could I tell you that would help you to trust me?"

- Questions which highlight what they need from work, for example: "Tell me about a good day at work?" "What gives you most satisfaction at work?" "What energises you?" "Tell me what a bad day at work looks like?" "What causes you most anxiety at work?" "What causes you to lose sleep at night?" "Which emotions do you experience most often?"

As you both open up more and reveal more to each other in response to specific questions, you may be able to use very open questions such as:

> "What one question could I ask you that would enable me to really understand you?"

When you know the other person well, also consider asking:

> "What one thing can you tell me that might be helpful for me to know about you that I don't already know?"

> "Do you have any unrealised ambitions?"

> "What do you most value about working here?"

> "What one thing would you change about working here and why?"

"What would you like to be most remembered for?"

D. Closing and following up

Close the conversation by:

- Summarising how you are similar to, and different from, each other; we know we feel more safe and secure when we find common ground with another person

- Asking your colleague how they found the conversation, and what benefits they feel they have gained

- Reciprocating with the benefits you feel you have gained, in terms of understanding them, and building a closer relationship with them

- Expressing your sincere thanks to your colleague for their openness and willingness to share their perspectives, values, preferences, etc.

After the conversation, make a point of following up with a face-to-face chat or phone call to repeat your thanks for their openness, and reiterating the benefits you believe you have both achieved from the conversation. Remember that this conversation isn't a one-off – have similar conversations at appropriate times in the future!

In summary

This conversation helps to lay the foundations for success in all the other conversations and interactions you will have with your colleague in the weeks and months ahead. It's about getting to know each other beyond the basics of families, vacations, sports and hobbies. It's driven by your genuine curiosity to know and understand your colleague at a deeper, more personal level. As you will have realised, this may not be a one-off conversation – you can return to it a number of times as your relationship develops, building a fuller picture of your colleague over time. The more you practise this conversation the more natural it will become. You will find it immensely rewarding not only to build deeper relationships with your colleagues, but also to be appreciated as a leader who takes a genuine, personal interest in their team members and colleagues at work.

CHAPTER 6

Conversation 2
Agreeing mutual
expectations

A client describes this experience at work:

I joined a company several years ago as global HR VP. The company is a global technology business employing nearly 50,000 people worldwide, with half of its staff now based in growth markets. It has a superb brand and reputation for innovative solutions and for employing the most creative and talented people.

However its financial performance over the past five years has been very average, with divisions in Europe and the US making losses, only surviving because of strong performances from its operations in growth markets. Over time it has evolved a very heavy and multi-layered system of corporate governance, with quite confused accountability for delivering business performance.

In previous roles I have been used to having a clear relationship with business leaders where there was real clarity on what I was accountable for delivering for the business and how it linked to an overall vision and strategy. Here we had vague and ill-defined values, but no real sense of drive and purpose.

Over the last few years I tried numerous times to get a clear sense of direction from the business and to connect what we were delivering from an HR perspective with what the business was trying to achieve. But in reality I was never able to have this conversation in a meaningful way because there was such a lack of leadership and accountability within the Ex Com.

In the end it became so frustrating that I decided I needed to get out and find a new role in a business that had a real sense of purpose and where I could be part of a team that had a shared sense of accountability for driving forward to achieve something meaningful and worthwhile. I'm pleased to say I joined my new company three months ago and it's so refreshing to be back in an environment in which there is clarity on what we are trying to achieve, why it matters and how we are working together as team to deliver a stretching business plan.

What this conversation is about

This conversation has two key elements: firstly, being clear with your colleagues not just about *what* you are seeking to achieve at work but also *why* it matters, and secondly, being clear about the *expectations* you can hold of colleagues in supporting you in achieving these outcomes. Equally it's an exploration of the same elements in their work: *what* are they seeking to achieve and *why* does it matter, and what *expectations* can they have of you in supporting them to achieve the outcomes they are working towards?

This conversation is therefore fundamentally about agreeing a motivating, two-way contract of mutual support between two people at work who are mutually dependent for success in achieving their goals –

and especially between a leader and each of their team members.

It's worth contrasting this conversation with the typical Performance Management discussion about objectives. In the best systems a set of clear objectives for each employee will be agreed at the start of the year, and the employee will have some input and discretion in shaping these objectives in discussion with their line manager. There may even be objectives for personal development included in the process. More typically, objectives are handed down to employees with little discussion or involvement and the process becomes a ritualised form-filling exercise. And in many organisations leaders freely admit that even this process does not happen consistently so that team members simply end up performing the same set of activities as the year before. And the process of objective-setting typically varies by function. In sales teams where it is relatively easy to set targets these are usually in place, whereas in support functions or engineering teams or R&D operations, where it's more difficult to set objectives, the process is often absent completely.

But what is lacking even in the best Performance Management processes are the two key elements in this conversation: discussion of *"purpose"* – the *why* you are seeking to achieve these specific outcomes, and the *expectations* that you can have of others to support you in achieving these outcomes.

Explicit discussion of purpose is rare in today's world of work. But as Simon Sinek powerfully points out in *Start with Why* [21], in order for people to be truly inspired at work they need to be able to engage with a greater purpose than simply the pursuit of profit. This conversation is about finding a way as a leader to articulate how what you are seeking to achieve contributes towards achievement of this higher purpose. It's about standing back from your day-to-day activities, asking yourself honestly what is really driving you to get out of bed in the morning, and being able to convey this to other people in an authentic, open manner.

Let's be clear here that we are not asking you to fabricate some over-arching, idealistic, altruistic purpose at work that sounds inspiring but has no actual basis in reality. You know enough about our in-built ability as human lie detectors to appreciate that that's never going to work. Few of us are really engaged in changing the world or saving the planet (although if you are, then find a way to articulate it)! From many thousands of conversations with real leaders at work we do know that when they have time to reflect, many are driven by strongly-held convictions to deliver exceptional service to customers, create truly innovative technical solutions, create secure employment opportunities for people in their teams, develop the next generation of engineers or scientists, develop life-changing drugs, provide great services to local communities and customers, and a hundred other genuine passions and causes. So part of the process to prepare for this conversation is to think deeply about what drives you to do what you do at work *beyond* the necessity to earn a living and bring in that monthly pay cheque.

The second component of this conversation is about 'the expectations I can have of you to support me in achieving my outcomes', and 'the expectations you can have of me in supporting you to achieve yours'. Here we are using the term "expectations" in its widest sense. There could be expectations of technical, financial or resource support. There could be expectations to influence others and provide moral support in meetings or negotiations. And there could be expectations to provide coaching, feedback and developmental support both to prepare for critical opportunities or interactions, and also to de-brief and learn from them afterwards.

Open, two-way discussion of purpose and expectations, as well as what you are both trying to achieve, builds mutual accountability for success and greatly contributes towards the ultimate goal of forging a trusting relationship in which team members feel proud to belong to the organisation, choose to go the extra mile and believe they can build a fulfilling career in the organisation.

So this conversation is not a substitute for the good Performance Management practice of setting and agreeing objectives; rather it is a conversation that can enhance and make this process so much richer, deeper and more meaningful.

This conversation also has an obvious application beyond a leader and members of their team. Whatever your leadership role there will be key individuals in other functions, as well as external customers, suppliers and other stakeholders who are vital in helping your deliver your business plan. Why wouldn't you deliberately plan to sit down with them too and hold this conversation and establish a similar contract of mutual support?

Why this conversation matters

This conversation matters because in today's world of work we are all mutually dependent. There are very few roles, let alone leadership roles, where you can achieve the outcomes you need to deliver without a whole range of people inside and outside your team also achieving what they need to achieve. If you lead a sales team, every member of your team needs to perform, as do those who manufacture or create what you sell, those who supply you and those who process invoices and deliver logistics. If you lead a finance team you are totally dependent on every team member delivering their part of the process, as well as the full spectrum of internal and external customers and suppliers doing the same.

Traditional Performance Management processes recognise this interdependence in the sense that objectives for each individual in each department or function, when aggregated into a single whole, should in theory add up to a set of activities that will deliver the business plan. But we know in real life it rarely works as smoothly as this, and given the complexity and rate of change we face today this is hardly surprising. This conversation makes it much more likely that the objectives which do emerge from the Performance Management process will be effective in delivering the business plan, for the following reasons:

- More trusting human relationships will start to be formed between the individuals and teams who are mutually dependent, enabling productive conversations to take place to manage the inevitable bottlenecks and pinch points caused by change and growth.

- As Stephen M.R. Covey notes in *The Speed of Trust* [22], it is trust that improves efficiency and reduces cost. And as people develop a sense of shared purpose they are more likely to adapt and flex their processes to help achieve a greater goal, rather than rigidly holding to out-dated processes that get in the way of service to customers and quality products and solutions.

- And finally, explicit discussion and agreement on mutual support creates the conditions in which people feel empowered to offer and receive the resources, time, coaching and feedback that contributes to getting the job done faster and to the quality levels required.

Why this conversation often does not happen at work

Why do we so rarely share (or even think about) that deeper sense of purpose that is driving us to do what we do as leaders at work? From the many thousands of conversations we have had with leaders at work we believe there are three major reasons. It's helpful to take each one in turn and reflect on what we can do to address it and therefore remove this barrier to undertaking this vital component of your role as a leader.

The first reason is the simplest: the relentless pace of activity that we face at work fills our time to capacity and denies us any space for reflection, or even planning and simple forward thinking. But getting into shape to hold these conversations effectively is a vital part of your role as a leader, and we hope you are convinced of this by now.

Secondly, we don't have a process for doing it: because it's often not recognised as a key part of our role as leader, we are unsure how to go about it. In the next section we will give you a simple process to get you started.

Thirdly, and perhaps most significantly, we may feel sceptical about the value of doing it at all. Because it's not about numbers, costs, revenues, metrics or KPIs (Key Performance Indicators), it feels soft and un-business-like. We may feel awkward about articulating something that we haven't tried to express before, and worry that our colleagues will poke fun at us for taking on a new form of "management speak". We will address this too in the next section, and help you to develop a mindset in which your sense of purpose takes centre stage and you can be authentic and honest in the way you express this to colleagues in one-to-one and group settings.

Another question is, why do we not discuss the expectations we have of each other at work to provide mutual support? The same explanations cited above probably also apply here, but we believe there is another fundamental reason at play too. To ask for support implies vulnerability, and that's something we are absolutely conditioned to avoid at work. A key part of your role as a leader through role modelling these conversations is to demonstrate that asking for and offering support to team members and colleagues is actually a demonstration of maturity and self-confidence, rather than an admission of weakness.

It's so common for people *not* to have this conversation, particularly senior leaders, who often think that their direct reports should know what to do just because they are senior themselves. As one of our colleagues saw, actually having a conversation about expectations can have a huge impact:

Pierre was a VP at a healthcare provider who was having problems with Maria, one of his direct reports, as she never produced what Pierre needed her to and never appeared to take any initiative. Pierre found this particularly irritating, as Maria was a senior manager and so should be proactive. Maria was frustrated as she felt that, whatever she did, it wasn't what Pierre wanted. Pierre's coach challenged him, "Have you specifically told Maria that you're expecting her not just to produce accurate reports but you also expect her to be proactive, take initiative and drive things forward?" Pierre's response was, "Well, she's a Director, she's paid enough, she should know what she's meant to be doing at that level."

The coach persuaded Pierre that it was worth having the conversation with Maria and being transparent about his expectations, and to use words like "I was expecting you to be comfortable at your level to take the initiative and find new ways of presenting our management information, and I'm feeling disappointed you haven't done that. I realise that I haven't been clear, and what I'd like is…" It was very out of character for Pierre to have this sort of conversation, and Maria was taken aback. However she responded positively and told Pierre that she hadn't realised that Pierre wanted her to be proactive – she'd thought that Pierre just liked telling her what to do. After this conversation Maria was very clear about what Pierre expected and her performance improved. On the occasions when she didn't meet Pierre's expectations, then Pierre could refer back to the conversation and they could have a constructive discussion about what needed to happen next.

Why this conversation works

This conversation works because it touches on three elements of the FIVEC model to create a positive, *towards* response.

In terms of Influence, the conversation is clearly an opportunity for an adult-to-adult interaction between you and a colleague in which there is a respectful, open, honest discussion of what you are both seeking to achieve, why it matters to you and how you can support each other.

Secondly, the conversation contributes directly to empowerment, as your team member will leave the conversation with a mandate to work towards the outcomes you have discussed, together with the moral and logistical support they need to be successful.

Finally, as a result of the conversation there will be increased clarity on what needs to be achieved and, importantly, why it matters. This creates a greater sense of groundedness which we know is vital for people to give their best at work.

Sabine was the Compliance Director for a major pharmaceutical company. She'd recently joined the company and was extremely knowledgeable about compliance, but was upsetting her colleagues. In particular, the company had recently had a reorganisation, where responsibilities for compliance worldwide had been divided between Sabine and Alex – both Directors. Sabine was an outspoken, fiery Dutch lady and Alex a reserved Swiss man; the two of them found each other impossible. Moreover, Sabine's direct style – where in conference calls she would say things like "that's ridiculous" or "you can't do that" – wasn't going down very well with colleagues in the USA. Sabine's boss really respected her expertise, but couldn't afford for her to keep upsetting people. The company had a well-established coaching programme for senior leaders, so Sabine was sent "to be coached"!

The coaching started with a 360 degree feedback questionnaire. When Sabine saw the feedback from her peers and team her initial reaction was to say "Well, I'll leave"! Having calmed down she was encouraged to think about how to make the most of the coaching and it was clear that her relationship with Alex was a key place to start, as it was critical that they should make the split of responsibilities work better. The coach encouraged Sabine to think about what Alex's strengths were and how best to have a conversation with him about their responsibilities. Alex was extremely organised and, although reserved, was very comfortable chairing meetings and agreeing processes. He was introverted and so needed time to reflect, whereas Sabine acted very much in the moment. So in order to get things going, Sabine invited Alex to a meeting, and highlighted the purpose (to agree how best to split their responsibilities between them) and gave him an agenda in advance, so that he had the opportunity to prepare before meeting her.

The coach helped Sabine think through what the meeting needed to cover:

How can we make our working relationship better? What would work for you? What are our expectations of each other? How can we divide the work to reflect our strengths and preferences? Let's acknowledge that things haven't worked as well in the past as they could have – if we were starting with a clean sheet of paper to plan how to work together, what would we do? How can we clear up any misunderstandings we may have between us?

The meeting went well; Alex appreciated the structure and they came to an agreement about how to work between themselves. He recorded the actions and is helping them keep on track. The agreement to split work in a way which played to each of their strengths gave them each things that they most enjoyed doing.

And the longer term impact? As well as finding a way for Sabine and Alex to work together, the experience has encouraged her to appreciate that people have different expectations of each other and she listens more to others' views, which has helped in her interactions with colleagues in the USA.

The practicalities of holding this conversation

A. Clarifying and articulating your sense of *purpose* – *why* you are doing what you are doing at work

We recommend you work through this simple three-stage model in order to clarify your sense of purpose:

1. Think about and write down the elements of your job where you feel most fulfilled, where it doesn't feel like "work", where you would be doing this anyway even if you weren't paid, that you care most about and talk about most

passionately, where you go the extra mile and put in the extra hours and effort, where you are at your most creative and engaged, when you feel at the top of your game

2. Think about and note down what you would like your legacy to be at work, how you would want to be remembered by team members and colleagues if you left your team or organisation tomorrow; this might be for what you have achieved, or how you achieved it, or what you stood for at work in terms of your values or impact on others

3. Finally, stand back and look at the big picture of what you are trying to achieve at work this year and identify which of your passions above are driving you towards these goals; find a trusted colleague and practise articulating the linkage between your goals and your drivers until it feels authentic, honest and comfortable

B. Identifying *who* to have the conversation with, and *why* and *when* it will be helpful

Think about the people with whom you have the closest mutual dependence in terms of achieving your goals over the months or year ahead. As the leader of a team it's likely that all of your direct reports fall into this category. Think about when it will be most beneficial to schedule the conversation. We recommend that this conversation is best held at the start of the Performance Management or business planning cycle, as a scene-setting exercise prior to the formulation of detailed business plans, budgets and objectives. Equally, as the leader of a new team, or as the manager of a new team member, the conversation can be helpful and useful at any stage of the Performance Management or business planning cycle.

Think about other colleagues at work where there is a high degree of mutual dependence and go through a similar exercise to plan when it would be most useful to hold this conversation with them.

C. Setting up the conversation and issuing an invitation to it

Every situation is unique, and each of us has our own preferred ways of working and communicating, but in all cases we recommend these three simple steps:

1. Identify the person you plan to have the conversation with

2. Send an invitation to the conversation, being conscious of how elements of the FIVEC model can accidentally cause an **away** reaction, and invite a response

   "Hi Peter – I'd like us to get together for a discussion about what we are both trying to achieve over the next 6 months / year, and how we can support each other to maximise our chances of being successful. I'll ask my PA to get a convenient time in our schedules over the next couple of weeks. Looking forward to catching up."

3. Prepare yourself to be at your best in the conversation, using the following steps:

a. Head: Am I really clear about my purpose and how we are mutually dependent?

b. Hand: Have I thought through, and planned, the agenda and questions that will be most helpful in making this conversation go well?

c. Heart: Have I found a way to express my purpose which is truly authentic and comfortable for me?

D. Planning the agenda for the conversation

The following statements and questions will be helpful; you may also find it useful to pass them to your colleague in advance of the conversation so that they can also be prepared:

"Let me give you an overview of what I'm trying to achieve over the next period, and especially why this matters for me ..."

"Can you talk me through the same thing from your point of view? What are you trying to achieve and why is it important to you?"

"So can we explore how we can support each other in achieving our goals?"

"How can I support you in terms of resources, influencing, coaching, etc.? What would be most helpful for you?"

"How do you think you can best support me?"

"How might we get in each other's way? Is there anything we should be aware of or avoid doing?"

"So can we summarise the expectations we have of each other, and how we can hold each other to account for delivering on these expectations?"

E.   Closing and following up

Close the conversation by:

- Asking your colleague how they found the conversation, and what benefits they feel they have gained

- Reciprocating with the benefits you feel you have gained, in terms of a clear understanding of what you are both trying to achieve, why it matters to both of you and the expectations you have of each other in providing mutual support

- Expressing your sincere thanks to your colleague for their openness and willingness to share their goals, purpose and expectations

After the conversation, make a point of following up with a face-to-face chat or phone call to repeat your thanks for their openness, and summarising your goals, purpose and mutual expectations of support. If there are specific actions you have agreed to, in order to help each other, remember to do so!

In summary

This is a vital conversation to have with everyone at work with whom you are mutually dependent for success in your job. It starts with you challenging yourself to articulate your "why" or sense of purpose. What's getting you out of bed in the morning and driving you to deliver the outcomes that are really important to you – and what expectations do you hold of your colleague in supporting you in this? Equally, how can you understand what's driving them and the expectations they have of you in helping them to achieve what they need to deliver at work? The conversation is driven by your intention to create clarity, a sense of empowerment and mutually assured success in your roles. It's an important opportunity for you to add real value as a leader.

CHAPTER 7

Conversation 3
Showing genuine
appreciation

Some years ago we were working with the Head of a major IT services company who made a sudden discovery about the unexpected consequences of his behaviour:

David was an extremely intelligent and capable individual, in his forties, who had been with the organisation for some time and risen through the ranks to the position of CEO.

He was known for his focus and grip on the business and determination for the organisation to be successful, which was demonstrated through a pacesetting leadership style. He deliberately chose to select and surround himself with bright, driven and self-motivated individuals and was at his most comfortable in group situations debating key ideas and strategies. This behaviour extended to the use of humour, often cutting, directed at others.

The irony is that David's heart and instinct was to care for and support others but the way he had chosen to achieve this was through a high-performance route. Those who did not fit into the mould would often be anxious and uncertain around him and so reinforce the perceptions he had of them in a self-fulfilling prophecy.

All this changed when one of his key direct reports decided to leave. Marcus had been a rising star, groomed for succession and apparently very similar in style to David. However, in a frank and open exchange Marcus revealed that a key criticism he had of David was his focus on the shortcomings and mistakes of others. "I know you have high standards, but over time the constant criticism has worn me down and I just don't have the energy to put up with it any more. With my own team I enjoy praising people when they do things well and spending time focusing on their strengths... but I've never seen you praise or thank anyone, no matter how well we've done."

This was a shock and a catalyst for David. He recognised that he was 'burning up' his people in an attempt to drive success, and he committed to spending more time with key members of his team one-to-one, exploring areas of strength and how to develop them even further, rather than focus on highlighting their shortcomings in a group situation.

Because of his style, this was something he stuck at and so over time the effect was transformational on both David and his team. It enabled him to hand over more accountability and ownership to his direct reports, revealed strengths in others he had not noticed before and changed the dynamic of team meetings.

His own comment was, "I'm beginning to realise that *my* way isn't *the* way and my job is to help others be the best they can be every day in *their* way."

What this conversation is about

When was the last time you showed genuine appreciation for someone's contribution at work? Sadly, if you are typical of most leaders, you may have to scratch your head and think back quite carefully over the past weeks or months. The reality is that taking the time to show genuine appreciation at work is a much neglected activity and most workplaces are the poorer for it.

This conversation is about focusing on what people are doing well at work and where they are being really successful. It's about exploring this situation with them, to understand how they are being successful and how their unique strengths and talents are contributing to their success. It's about showing genuine appreciation for their efforts and contribution. And it's about exploring the potential to make more of these strengths and talents in other aspects of their work, or elsewhere in the organisation, to develop their performance and benefit the business. And fundamentally it's about drawing learning and insights from the situation, and your team member's performance, in order to further improve performance in the future.

And of course it's also about "catching people doing something right" in the moment, and showing genuine, heartfelt, spontaneous appreciation.

We make a distinction between a *planned, exploratory* discussion to focus on where a team member is being really successful, and *spontaneous* gratitude in the moment for something you personally see going well, for the following reason. In today's world of work with dispersed global teams and virtual working, you will often not be personally present to witness it at first hand when your team member has a success or demonstrates some really positive behaviours. So without the planned discussion to explore what is going well for them, you may never create the opportunity to give them the recognition they deserve, nor be able to help them draw the learning from it which will sustain high performance in the future.

This conversation is also about showing that you care about not just the *performance* of your people but also about their *emotional* well-being. When people talk to you about what's going well for them, their stories will often be about the challenges they have overcome in dealing with difficult situations with other people both within your business and beyond it – customers, suppliers, other stakeholders. This conversation is a vital opportunity for you to empathise with their experiences and feelings – to demonstrate that you appreciate how challenging it sometimes is to stand in their shoes.

This conversation deliberately borrows from the concept and process of Appreciative Inquiry (AI), more commonly used as a method for identifying organisational strengths. The idea behind AI is that in the western world we have defaulted into a "deficiency" model of analysis in which our starting point is always to look for what's wrong so that we can fix it. AI offers an alternative approach in which the analysis starts with what's working well and then asks how we can build on these strengths. The original article on AI published in 1987 by David Cooperrider and Suresh

Srivastva [23] argued that the over-use of a problem-solving approach in trying to improve the performance of groups, organisations and communities reduces the ability of leaders to see opportunities for improvement through innovation and growth. They argue that the questions we ask tend to focus our attention in a particular direction. When the questions asked are "What's wrong?" and "What needs to be fixed?" the obvious assumption is that something is wrong and that something needs to be fixed. AI is underpinned by an alternative belief that every organisation, and every person in that organisation, has positive aspects that can be built upon. So AI starts with questions such as "What's working well?" and "What's good about what you are currently doing?"

Appreciative Inquiry
• What's working well?
• What's good about what we are doing?

Traditional deficiency model
• What's wrong?
• What needs to be fixed?

Some researchers believe that excessive focus on deficiencies actually causes people to perform worse, or at least fail to improve. By contrast, AI argues that when all members of an organisation are motivated to understand and value the most positive features of its culture or people, it can make rapid improvements.

We observe the exact same limitation with the idea of "feedback" or "constructive criticism" which is so prevalent in leadership teaching today. Worse, use of feedback that focuses on deficiencies tends to generate defensiveness in those receiving it, and anxiety in those giving it. (Of course, it is sometimes necessary to challenge a colleague's unhelpful behaviour, and we tackle this head on in the next chapter.)

Another deliberate feature of this conversation is that it focuses exclusively on strengths and what's going well. Leaders who attend a workshop to learn about and practise the 5 Conversations are often astonished when the facilitators run this conversation at the front of the room and it ends having only covered what's gone well. Frequently several people will call out, "Hey, where's the criticism? We were waiting for you to get to the negative feedback! You can't leave it there!" "What about the praise sandwich of Praise – Criticism – Praise?!" This leads into a discussion of how their culture seems always to focus on the deficiency model – people have weaknesses and the leader's job is to tell people about them and fix them. But remember this conversation is about drawing *learning* from success, so often the discussion will also embrace situations that have gone less well but from which learning has been drawn that did lead in the end to a successful outcome.

Finally, this conversation is about attaching emotion and feelings to the statement of appreciation. Don't fake it if you don't really feel it, but most leaders who take the trouble to understand how and why a team member is being successful come to feel that they are genuinely grateful, not only for the skills and talents their team member has deployed but also for the hard work and commitment they have demonstrated too. There is no harm, and lots to be gained, from expressing this emotion as you say "Thank you".

Spontaneous appreciation matters too. When you do witness a colleague being successful, resolving a problem or helping a colleague, seize the moment to show genuine appreciation. Say "Well done!" and "Thank you!" and "I really appreciate what you've just done!" Spot it. Feel it. Share it.

Why this conversation matters

We know that people need to feel valued at work in order to give their best. And they need to feel they are contributing to something worthwhile and making a difference. There is no more powerful way to achieve this than you giving them your full attention to really explore their achievements and why and how they are being successful. And don't forget there is a physical effect in people when they are shown genuine appreciation and trust; it triggers the brain to release dopamine – which makes them feel good.

People also benefit from building their self-confidence at work. We are all our own harshest critics and often take for granted the things we do well. This conversation helps your team member to understand their strengths, and deepens their self-awareness of not only what they are achieving, but also how they are being successful. Remember this conversation is about drawing learning from success, and often from the journey of setbacks that led there too.

All of this contributes to people feeling that they are learning, growing and improving at work and in their career. In Daniel Pink's terms[20], they are moving towards mastery in their role, a powerful human need that we seek to satisfy at work if we have the opportunity.

Apart from benefits to the individual from holding this conversation, there are major benefits for you and for your organisation. For you as a leader you learn about the qualities of your people, and build deeper and more trusting relationships with them. You learn how to deploy them to achieve greater personal success as a leader, and you build loyalty and engagement within your team that will contribute to sustained high performance.

Just as important, but less obvious, these discussions give you vital insights and a deeper understanding of the challenges facing your team out there in the real world. You can't be alongside every one of your team each day to witness the challenges they face at first hand, but you can learn much about these challenges and opportunities through this conversation. You will gain valuable insights that will enable you to drive innovation and continuous improvement.

Finally, the business benefits from understanding the hidden potential and wider talent pool it has within. Rather than relying on external recruitment, it starts to be possible to develop an internal talent pipeline as you and your colleagues come to deeply understand the true potential of your people.

Why this conversation often does not happen at work

There are many factors that get in the way of this conversation happening at work. Here are a few that come up most often, and some possible ways to overcome them.

The first touches on a reaction we mentioned earlier, of astonishment that it's legitimate just to have a conversation about what's going well without adding in a number of criticisms and examples of poor performance. Many leaders are genuinely taken aback that we advocate this conversation at all. But recall that this conversation explores the journey towards success, and often this involves learning from setbacks or situations your team member will often readily volunteer they have handled less well and therefore learnt from. The big difference is that your team member will reflect on these situations and their learning themselves. They are not the passive recipients of criticism from you, which will inevitably cause defensiveness and an *away from* reaction. (However, as we mentioned earlier, when an individual has demonstrated unhelpful behaviour it is important that this is faced up to, and this is the subject of our next chapter.)

Another reason often cited as to why this conversation does not happen is expressed as the belief "People are paid for the work they do. Why should say I 'thank you' to them?" Hopefully by now you will have no problem in refuting this argument. It is true that we all get paid for the work we do. But our salary is only one component of the psychological contract we have with our employer. Just as important are the relationships we have at work, the opportunities for learning and growth, the satisfaction of achieving and winning, the sense of contributing towards a greater purpose. This conversation is a vital contribution towards all these deeper reasons why we remain engaged at work and commit to build our career with the organisation. A company where leaders believe that all they need to provide is a pay cheque each month is unlikely to be one with high engagement and superior business performance.

If leaders have not been used to holding this type of conversation, they may also feel awkward about it and worry that they will come across as insincere. The workshop that we run on holding these conversations provides leaders with an opportunity to practise this conversation with a colleague, and without fail leaders report that it was easier and more natural than they expected. The key is to develop a mindset of genuine curiosity about how your team member achieved success, and to follow a simple process that we set out below.

Why this conversation works

This conversation is powerful because it touches on two of the elements of the FIVEC model.

Firstly it demonstrates how you as a leader value your team member and the contribution they are making. Listening with genuine interest, and using probing questions to explore how they have met their challenges at work and used their skills and talent to be successful, will show how deeply you value their contribution and generate a *towards* response.

This conversation also contributes towards a sense of empowerment as you endorse and support their ability to act even more autonomously in the future, using their skills and talents to handle even more challenging situations.

A group of our colleagues got together to brainstorm ideas for a new training course. They were running through different sections of the course and Pat came up with a few ideas. James said, "Pat, it's fantastic working with you, you're so creative!" Pat was puzzled, "Really?" "Yes, you're always coming up with great new ways of doing things" said another one in the group.

Pat felt great; she'd been recognised by her colleagues and just hadn't expected it. Not only had the praise come out of the blue, but also she'd never thought of herself as being creative.

This spontaneous appreciation didn't just have an immediate impact on Pat; it had a longer-lasting effect. Having been told by her peers that she was creative, Pat thought of herself differently. It was as if she'd been told that it's OK to be creative. She felt motivated to do similar work and now actively seeks out opportunities to create new training designs.

The practicalities of holding the planned, exploratory conversation

A. Identifying *who* to have the conversation with, and *when* it will be helpful

We recommend that you aim to hold this conversation with every member of your team, several times per year. If you have a monthly or bi-monthly catch-up session with members of your team, why not make it the default starting point for the conversation? For all the reasons discussed above it will be a motivating and insightful place to start your meeting.

B. Setting up the conversation

You can consciously plan to hold the conversation as described above, and doing so in this way is important to ensure that it does happen systematically and consistently.

It's also powerful and effective to be more spontaneous in having the conversation. One leader said to us:

> I often find myself visiting sales offices in the various countries I travel to. I always make the effort to walk around and chat to the desk-based team. What a great idea it would be to ask them "What's going really well for you at the moment?" I've never done that before but I can really see how it will open up a great conversation with them!

Prepare yourself personally for the conversation by focusing on the following areas:

- Each member of your team comes to work with a positive intent – to do the best they can for their colleagues and their customers. They face challenges every day at work and they overcome them using their skills, talents and emotional resilience

- This is your opportunity to say "Thank You!" for the commitment and effort that people make on your behalf

- It's OK to invest your emotions and feelings in this discussion – feel for your colleague and make your appreciation genuine and from the heart

C. Planning the agenda for the conversation

The following structure and questions are recommended for this conversation:

1. Understand and appreciate

    a. What's going really well for you at the moment? What's been your biggest success in the last few weeks? What's been your biggest achievement recently? What's been your biggest challenge?

    b. What was the situation? What were the key challenges you faced?

    c. What did you say and do that led to success?

    d. How did you feel as this was happening?

e. What strengths, talents and skills of yours contributed most to this outcome?

f. What's the learning you take from this experience?

g. How are you feeling right now?

h. Thank You! I want you to know that I really appreciate the contribution you are making, and the skills and commitment you are bringing to our team

2. Explore

a. What other opportunities are there for you to use these strengths, talents and skills?

b. How else can we play to your strengths?

c. How do you want to develop these skills further?

3. Consolidate

a. What's the key insight you have gained from this discussion?

b. What learning points should we both take away?

c. What are the action points that we both commit to follow up on?

D. Closing and following up

After the conversation, make a point of following up with a face-to-face chat or phone call to repeat your thanks for their contribution and the skills and strengths they are deploying. If you've agreed specific actions you have committed to follow up on, remember to do so!

Showing spontaneous appreciation

By definition you don't plan for these conversations as they are expressions of appreciation in the moment. In our experience leaders often hold back from doing this because they wish to appear to be fair and balanced with all of their team members or to have time to write down and rehearse what they want to say. In our view this is a distorted logic. We believe that the rewards to be gained by spontaneously and authentically showing pleasure and appreciation for what colleagues do will, over time, be valued and respected far more by *all* of the team.

When we run the 5 Conversations programme we have a session where we encourage anyone in the room to give some spontaneous appreciation to another person in the room for something that they have done that day or recently. There are always people who stand up and do so, but unlike some other training courses, not everyone does or has to. As a result some people offer appreciation and sometimes one person receives more than one acknowledgement. Whether people give it, receive it or neither, the effect on everyone in the room is amazingly powerful due to the genuine, spontaneous and authentic nature of the session.

So what you can do is develop a mindset in which, every day, you will identify something positive in the work and behaviour of your team members and colleagues. Be prepared to call it in the moment and to show in what you say and do that it's something you really value and appreciate.

In summary

We all need to know that our contribution is valued at work. Feeling appreciated is fundamental to our sense of well-being and fulfilment. This conversation ensures that every member of your team experiences these emotions several times a year. But more than this, it ensures that you deeply understand the unique strengths and talents that every member brings to your team. Not only does this enable you to ensure they play to their strengths and make your team stronger, but also gives you a vital insight into the depth of talent you and your organisation have access to. And holding these conversations will also give *you* a deep sense of fulfilment from having given people the recognition that they deserve.

CHAPTER 8

Conversation 4
Challenging unhelpful
behaviour

A consultant describes this experience with one of her clients:

Jo was working as a consultant with the CEO of an insurance company and his team of direct reports. The team was having a really tough time. There appeared to be a lot of in-fighting and the team just wasn't performing effectively. The CEO was very concerned and determined to do something about it, and he felt that the team really needed to understand how to work together. So he brought in a specialist training company to run a workshop on teamworking, he scheduled training in conflict management and he brought in some coaching. The training came and went and still the team was unable to perform effectively. What was going wrong?

When Jo had discussions with each of the team members about what was working and what wasn't working, a common theme emerged. It wasn't that they didn't know how to work together as a team or that they didn't want to work together, but instead there were a couple of team members whose behaviour wasn't being held to account. One in particular was extremely good at his job and wielded a lot of power, but wanted more control; as a consequence his style of operating was to bully and manipulate the others. And what was the team leader – the CEO – doing about this? Nothing. As far as the rest of his team could see, he was allowing this type of behaviour to happen, as if it were perfectly acceptable. This was what was holding the team back from working together effectively.

Jo fed this back to the CEO. The CEO had thought that *his team* needed training so that they could work together. Actually what was needed was for *the CEO* to do something different and challenge the unhelpful behaviour that everyone else could see was happening.

What this conversation is about

This conversation is about having the courage, insights and resources to face up to another person's unhelpful behaviour in such a way that you achieve a positive outcome for everyone involved, and emerge from the process with positive, even reinforced and deeper, trusting relationships. Does this sound challenging? Most leaders would agree that it does, and in our experience this is the conversation they feel they most need support with.

It isn't about the small tasks and behavioural things that come along day to day and which should be dealt with in the moment. It is about significant failures in performance or behaviour and where there is a recurrent unhelpful pattern of behaviour which becomes a problem.

This conversation starts with you as a leader recognising and acknowledging (even just to yourself) that a colleague is demonstrating unhelpful behaviour:

- Sometimes the behaviour may be unhelpful just for the individual concerned – mismanaging their workload so that they have to work late and damaging their work-life balance

- Sometimes the behaviour may be unhelpful just for you – a needy colleague who demands excessive amounts of your time complaining about minor issues they have with colleagues

- Sometimes the behaviour is self-evidently unhelpful for everyone concerned – being rude or abusive to you or other people

- It could be with clients, not listening to their needs, interrupting in meetings, being unreliable and failing to meet deadlines

- At other times the unhelpful behaviour will be less blatant but may be persistent and annoying to you and others – being consistently negative about ideas for change or improvement, holding on to a point of view or opinion when a group has moved on, supporting decisions in a meeting but not taking ownership for them later

It will be a rare team which does not encounter such behaviour at least periodically within the group, or in dealing with colleagues or contacts externally. And when this unhelpful behaviour is encountered it is a key part of your role as a leader to deal with it.

So this conversation is firstly about you having the courage to have a conversation with a team member or colleague to face up to their unhelpful behaviour.

The structure and mindset that we describe in this chapter offers a way for you to approach and manage this conversation that should reduce your anxiety and make it more likely you will feel able to tackle this type of issue. And of course, when you tackle unhelpful behaviour and achieve a positive outcome it can lead to a deeper relationship with your colleague and enhance your reputation as a fair and courageous leader.

This conversation is also about respect. It is respectful of your team members whose lives are being impacted negatively by their colleague's unhelpful behaviour. And it should also be motivated by respect for your colleague who is showing this unhelpful behaviour in the sense that you genuinely want to help them be successful at work, and in order to become so they need to change aspects of the behaviour they are demonstrating.

The structure that we recommend for this conversation is based on the principles of "Non Violent" or "Compassionate" Communication first developed by Marshall Rosenberg [24] as a means of disseminating peace-making skills during the civil rights movement in the US in the 1960s and which has been further developed since then. We believe the principles and process of Non Violent Communication (NVC) are a powerful and underused approach for dealing positively with unhelpful behaviour in the workplace. NVC offers a process and a mindset for honestly expressing your own feelings and needs, asking for a change in someone else's behaviour, and throughout maintaining a positive and respectful personal relationship. NVC is based on three underlying principles:

- The first principle is the importance of developing and acknowledging your own inner feelings. Rather than ignoring the impact of someone's unhelpful behaviour on you, or allowing it to constantly disrupt your focus and concentration on more important issues, it means acknowledging that it is there and owning your reaction to it, rather than blaming the other person.

- The second principle is about listening to your colleague with the intention to support them. This means appreciating that there are issues in your colleague's work, life and make up that are causing this behaviour which are real for them, and are almost certainly not malicious. Very few people demonstrate unhelpful behaviour with the conscious intention to hurt or annoy others.

- The third principle is about expressing your own feelings and needs, and acknowledging the feelings and needs of others in an authentic manner that will inspire understanding and respect, and is therefore likely to be reciprocated.

Taken together these three principles offer an approach to challenging unhelpful behaviour which is straightforward, honest and powerful. In practice the process, and the conversation derived from it, has four stages:

The NVC model

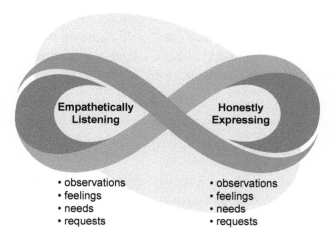

Empathetically
Listening

Honestly
Expressing

• observations
• feelings
• needs
• requests

• observations
• feelings
• needs
• requests

1. Observations

This stage is about talking about facts and observations in a non-threatening, non-judgemental way. It's about describing the behaviour that you have observed or experienced in as much detail, and with as much context, as you can provide. Sometimes these observations will be of behaviour you have witnessed at first hand yourself; at other times as a leader you will be discussing observations that other people have described to you. You may have notes to refer to so that you can be clear and accurate in what you are saying.

During this phase and subsequent phases you will invite a response from your colleague. How do they see the situation? Do they recognise the behaviour you are describing?

Your objective at this point is to try to keep the conversation focused on the facts. If, as is likely, the conversation moves on to the causes of the situation and their behaviour ("It wasn't my fault", "He did this to provoke me", "You never listen to me"), you need to gently but firmly say that "we'll come on to that in a moment, but first I'd like to talk about the impact of this behaviour I have observed".

Invite a response from your colleague on their perspective on the situation or on what has happened.

2. Feelings

This stage is about honestly expressing the feelings that your colleague's behaviour has caused in you or others. The use of the word "feeling" is deliberate and important. This is not about expressing your thoughts, analysis, conclusions or solutions. It is about authentically describing how your colleague's words or actions have caused you to feel. This is because these feelings are real, owned by you and therefore valid and important; a colleague could challenge any conclusions you come to, but they can't challenge how they have made you feel, whether it's disappointed, confused, irritated, upset, discouraged, uncertain, vulnerable, etc.

It is important at this stage to invite a response from your colleague about how they were feeling at the time, as well as how they are feeling now. It is also important at this stage to discuss the *reasons* for your colleague's feelings and behaviour.

3. Needs

At this stage you move the discussion on to the needs that you have as a leader and colleague so they can understand where and how the dissonance has arisen. So to take the examples of unhelpful behaviour mentioned earlier, your needs may be:

- To **support and protect** your staff so that they look after their health more, and achieve a better work-life balance by leaving work on time so they spend more time with their family

- For **respect** so that they stop complaining to you about the minor personal issues they have with their colleagues

- For **harmony** in the team and for them to build positive, respectful relationships with their colleagues

- for **reassurance** that they will take the time and effort to understand the needs of their clients

- for **support** from them by making a positive contribution in meetings and respecting the decisions made by the group

Invite your colleague to comment on your position, and also to express any needs that are important to them.

4. Requests

Finally in the process you make a clear request of your colleague and invite a response. To follow through with the examples above, requests could be stated as follows:

"So my request of you is that you…"

- Take the time to plan your workload at the start of each week, and flag to me if it's excessive so that we can work together to spread it out more evenly, or find extra resources if necessary

- Have open and honest conversations with your colleagues when you feel there is an issue between you, and only involve me if you have done this and it remains unresolved

- Make the effort to sit down with Jane and apologise for having offended her, and agree how you will work together more closely and respectfully in future

- Hold back on giving your opinions to clients early on in meetings, and use open-ended and probing questions to uncover their real needs and concerns

- Recognise that other people can perceive you to be forceful and dominant in meetings, and consciously encourage other people to share their ideas and views

Finally, invite your colleague to say if they have any requests to make of you.

It's worth mentioning that we have deliberately avoided using the word "feedback" to describe what this conversation is about. The skill of "giving feedback" is widely taught to leaders. Being ready to give feedback and having the skill to do it effectively are typically seen as positive characteristics of effective leaders.

However, David Rock, co-founder of the NeuroLeadership Institute, has tellingly written that, "In most people, the question 'can I offer you some feedback' generates a similar response to hearing fast footsteps behind you at night." [25]

In other words we have come to associate the phrase "giving feedback" with receiving criticism, the equivalent as far as the brain is concerned as being threatened or attacked, so provoking a strong *away from* response.

Another problem with feedback as it is conventionally delivered is that, unlike NVC, leaders are taught not to invest any of their own feelings into the process. Because it is delivered as a transactional, analytical process of observation, analysis and requirement for behaviour change, we do not believe it is likely to result in an emotional commitment to sustained change. (Having said that, we would rather this model of feedback is deployed if the alternative is not tackling the issue at all.)

Why this conversation matters

We have all seen the consequences when unhelpful behaviour goes unchallenged. Resentment grows, relationships deteriorate and soon quality and service suffer as internal conflict starts to get in the way of serving customers and delivering high performance.

When a team member's behaviour is unhelpful, his or her colleagues expect that, as the leader, you will tackle the problem honestly and openly. Doing so in a proactive and timely manner shows respect for the team and boosts your reputation as a fair and courageous leader. Ignoring the issue, or delaying facing it until the problem has become really serious, risks undermining the morale of the team and damaging team performance.

Why is unhelpful behaviour not challenged more often at work?

The main reason that unhelpful behaviour often goes unchallenged is that the prospect of facing up to a difficult conversation causes fear in the leader. Whilst some leaders say they have no problem with tackling this type of issue, our experience is that the majority do not relish the prospect, and for this reason these conversations are often put off longer than they should be, or avoided altogether. We know from the FIVEC model that the prospect of holding this conversation can cause an *away from* response in us. We fear damaging our relationship with our colleague by creating a barrier between us. We fear provoking a hostile reaction that will be unpleasant to deal with. We worry that they will feel unvalued or unfairly treated and that this will damage our reputation with colleagues or other members of our team.

We have seen above how the use of the NVC model offers a structure for the conversation that overcomes these barriers and is likely to lead to a win-win outcome.

Take the example of one of our colleagues Karen, who some years ago was working as a mid-level business partner in a chemicals business. One of her internal clients, Roberto, the Head of Finance and Administration, appeared to deliberately create anxiety and stress in others. Roberto's behaviour was controlling, unemotional, challenging and superior, not just to Karen but to everyone.

Although much more junior in status and age, Karen felt so provoked following one unpleasant encounter that at their next meeting, with her heart in her mouth, she said:

"I need to tell you that I find it very difficult working with you in that I don't feel you respect or encourage my contributions."

The effect was powerful, leading to a discussion about their respective roles and needs. It emerged that what Roberto valued most in others was technical expertise and what Karen most wanted was to be acknowledged and listened to. This provided a platform for much more open and equal discussions going forward.

Why this conversation works

The conversation is likely to be effective because it avoids blaming the other person for the impact of their behaviour and therefore does not have the effect of devaluing them as a person. It is also respectful of their positive intent and seeks to understand the underlying causes of their words and actions. It contributes to clarity by framing the outcome as a request for a specific change of behaviour that both parties can commit to work towards.

Finally, done authentically, talking honestly with someone about something that matters to you both can actually deepen a relationship rather than damage it.

An executive coach described what happened to one of her coachees, Christine, who led the Finance function for the EMEA region of a leisure company. One day Christine came straight to a coaching session from a team meeting, very upset and angry as one of her team, Sara, had been rude to her in front of everyone else. She really wanted to take it up with Sara and tell her off. "The behaviour had been unacceptable and needs to be challenged – right?"

Her coach encouraged her to think through how she was going to respond, rather than shoot from the hip. First of all she encouraged Christine to reflect on why the situation had upset her so much, and Christine revealed that she felt that she'd been shown a complete lack of respect, and respect was one of the values that were most critical to her. In addition, the culture she was working in was very status-conscious and she felt that her status was being undermined. Having identified that deep value, the coach questioned whether Christine's telling-off would be likely to show respect to Sara. Christine realised that if she wanted her team to treat her with respect then she needed to role model respect in what she did – even when challenging others. Her coach also asked what Christine wanted to get out of the conversation; she realised that she wanted Sara to realise why she was angry and that she didn't want it to happen again. At the same time she wanted to have a positive relationship with Sara moving forward, rather than their relationship getting worse as a result of the conversation.

Christine had the conversation with Sara. She told her how she felt about Sara's behaviour and then asked a critical question: what was going on for her? She then listened to Sara's emotions coming back; earlier in the meeting Sara had asked about the mobile phone policy and Christine had dismissed the query... which had led to Sara's outburst. Christine then asked Sara why she was concerned about the mobile phone policy and listened to Sara's concern about needing more training and there being no budget. By the end of the meeting both understood where the other was coming from and as a result their relationship improved.

Christine had wanted to challenge Sara's behaviour. By understanding the reasons behind her own emotions at the situation and thinking through what she wanted to achieve through that challenge, Christine went into the conversation with a more positive mindset which then got her the results both she and Sara needed.

The practicalities of holding this conversation

A. Identifying *who* to have the conversation with, and *when* it will be helpful

As soon as you observe or hear about an example of unhelpful behaviour you should take it up with the individual on the same day. If the unhelpful behaviour is not serious and you don't have the opportunity to have the conversation face-to-face on the same day, but will have the opportunity in the next two or three days, you may choose to delay it for a short period. However, if the delay is any longer than this we recommend you have the conversation quickly, by phone or Skype.

The only other reason to delay is if the unhelpful behaviour is being reported to you by a third party; in which case you may need to talk to other people who have been involved in an incident or relationship to hear their version of events.

B. Setting up the conversation and issuing an invitation

The exact form of words you use to set up the conversation needs to be tailored to the situation. In the case of a team member who is working long hours because of poor work planning you may simply bring the matter up in a regular catch-up meeting. Where the unhelpful behaviour is more serious, for example with an individual who has been abusive to you or a colleague, you definitely need to flag the reason for asking for the meeting in the invitation. Ideally the invitation will be made face-to-face, or if not left via voicemail, text or email.

"David, I would like us to get together to talk about how that meeting went yesterday. Can we meet at 2.00pm today in Conference Room 4?"

Prepare yourself personally for the conversation by focusing on the agenda below and working out the statements you will use and the questions you will ask.

C. Planning the agenda for the conversation

1. Observations

"David, I'd like to discuss the way you referred to me in the Marketing meeting yesterday."

"Do you remember saying to me that I wouldn't have anything to contribute to the discussion because, as a non-lawyer, the issues would be too complicated for me to understand?"

"What was your recollection?"

2. Feelings

"I must say that I felt hurt by this, especially because you said it in a public forum."

"How were you feeling at the time?"

"How are you feeling now?"

"What caused you to say that?"

"What's behind this?"

3. Needs

"I have a need to be treated with respect and to feel that my contribution is valued by you."

"What needs do you have?"

4. Requests

"My request of you is that in future you don't make negative comments about me in public."

"Will you be able to do this?"

"Are there any requests you would like to make of me?"

We're not used to expressing our feeling and needs at work and so often find it difficult to find the right words. The Center for Nonviolent Communication has produced useful inventories of words that express a wide range of feelings and needs, which are reproduced in the conversation toolkit at the back of this book – look this up to identify which words best describe what you're trying to convey.

D.   Closing

With this conversation in particular we believe that a short discussion at the end to 're-boot' the relationship is useful. This takes the form of standing back from the conversation itself, checking in with each other and reconnecting.

"I want to thank you for how you engaged with me on this."

"I appreciate the way you have approached this and hope you found it useful too."

"I'm pleased we have the kind of relationship where we can talk about how we feel and what we need."

This conversation is less likely to need structured follow-up unless the pattern of behaviour continues; in which case it needs to be revisited. On the other hand a positive shift in behaviour is a perfect opportunity for a spontaneous show of genuine appreciation!

In summary

This conversation starts from your deep sense of respect for the individual concerned, their colleagues and for yourself. However, you are in good company if the prospect of holding this conversation causes you to feel uneasy. But the structure we cover above offers you a route through the process that minimises these feelings and offers the best chance of a positive outcome. You can plan to be clear about the observations you will share and the legitimate feelings you attach to them. You can plan to ask for a response from your colleague. You can plan to describe the needs that you have and the request that you are making as a result, and again you can plan to ask for a response from your colleague. You will gain respect from your colleague for tackling the issue, and enhance your reputation as a leader prepared to face up to challenging situations. And the chances are that you *will* achieve the change in behaviour you are looking for.

CHAPTER 9

Conversation 5
Building for the future

A client, HR VP for a giant industrial conglomerate based in the Middle East, tells an apocryphal story:

Eight years ago we needed to appoint a new Group CFO based here in Dubai. We went out to our MDs and HR teams across the business to seek suitable internal candidates but after waiting for several weeks, and prompting a number of times, it was obvious that no internal candidates were forthcoming.

We decided to use an executive search firm and appointed a well-known, global firm of head hunters to work on the project. As usual the fees were huge – around US$250,000. They took the brief, wrote up the job description and created with us a person specification that exactly matched our requirements, and then set to work. As the weeks passed we received regular progress reports as they interviewed and shortlisted likely candidates.

Finally, eight weeks into the search process, the lead consultant scheduled to meet me. I was surprised when he entered my office to present his shortlist and declared that they had a bit of a problem and were concerned about how I was going to react. I was puzzled but said, "Go ahead and tell me what the issue is". This is what he said.

"We've completed our search for your new CFO, looking at candidates across the world with the industry experience that you are seeking and we have a shortlist of three people, and one candidate who is our strongest recommendation. There's only one problem. She's already employed by you."

They explained what had happened. Because our group is so diverse, some consultants on the search team in Europe did not realise that the companies they were searching in were part of our group. One of them found this strong candidate, but of course did not reveal to her who the search was on behalf of until after the second interview, by which time they were already certain she was a very strong candidate. Of course when she did hear who the search was for she was shocked too that it had taken an external search firm to identify her for an internal role! The outcome is that we did indeed appoint her as CFO, a post which she still fulfils very effectively today – and it cost us a lot of money!

But the deeper lesson is obvious, and what a wake-up call it was for us, and how embarrassing. Ever since then we have invested heavily in proper, deep career discussions with all of our key people to make sure this never happens again and that we have a sure grasp of the talent we have inside the organisation, and people's career goals.

What this conversation is about

Do you know the future dreams and career aspirations of your key people as well as the head hunter does? If you are a manager of managers, one thing you can be sure of is that many of your key people will be periodically contacted by head hunters and recruitment agencies, and from time to time they will meet them. You've probably done it yourself, and so you know what happens in these meetings.

Your key people will have poured their hearts out to the head hunter – what they love about their jobs, and what they dislike; what they want to do next in their career in terms of future roles and new challenges; where they want to be in three to five years' time and the development opportunities and experiences they need to get there. Wouldn't it be invaluable for you and your organisation to have access to this information?

This conversation is about gaining access to exactly these insights by having an open, adult-to-adult conversation with your team member. We acknowledge that it may be idealistic to believe that your team member will tell you absolutely everything they would say in confidence to an independent person outside their organisation; but our conviction and experience is that having built a trusting relationship, and using the structure recommended below, you can get 95% of the way there. And 95% is good enough to ensure that very few people will leave your organisation without you having exhausted every possible opportunity to enable them to build and fulfil their career ambitions within your organisation.

This conversation is about where your team member wants to be in three to five years from now against ten key dimensions. We have found that these ten dimensions cover all the major areas in which most people think about their careers, but we don't claim they are definitive; if different, additional areas matter to your colleague then talk about these too.

An important point to make up front is that this is not primarily a conversation about promotion. It may be an ambition of your team member to be promoted, or attain a particular level of seniority, status and reward with the organisation, and if this is the case they should tell you and you should listen and acknowledge their objective. It is important information for you and your organisation to be aware of. But the majority of the conversation is about the nature of the role and responsibilities they are seeking, and how you can take steps right now, in their current role, or through a change of job role in the coming months or years, to enable them to move towards this goal and get the career experiences they need to achieve it.

As the CEO of a Fortune 500 company said to his team during a 5 Conversations workshop,

"We are growing and changing so fast that whether the job titles of our key people change or not, the content of their jobs will be completely different in five years' time from what they are now. We must have this conversation with every one of them now so that they know they have the opportunity to build their careers with us."

Here are the ten dimensions we recommend using as a structure for this conversation.

1. Purpose / Meaning

This dimension concerns the degree to which an individual is driven by the need to have a clear line of sight between their role and contribution and a meaningful end goal that is greater than themselves. People who are driven by a sense of purpose seek organisations and roles in which they feel they can make a difference to the people, wider society and world around them.

2. Autonomy / Freedom

Wanting autonomy and freedom is about seeking a role in which you have a high degree of freedom to act, control of your own job content and working hours, and the ability to shape the future of your team, function and business.

3. Mastery / Learning

People who seek mastery and learning are driven by the need to be developing and continuously improving in their role at work.

4. Innovation / Exploration

This dimension is about having opportunities for creativity, discovery, innovation and exploration within the role.

5. Collaboration / Inclusivity

People for whom this dimension is important seek opportunities to work or lead in teams where working closely with other people is a key element of the role.

6. Achievement / Recognition

This dimension concerns an individual's needs to be able to win, succeed and achieve and to do so in an environment in which this success is visible, recognised and rewarded.

7. Work-Life Balance / Wellbeing

This is about an individual's needs to balance their time and effort at work with a fulfilling and meaningful life outside work with family and friends, along with a concern for their own physical, mental and emotional state.

8. Advancement / Promotion

This dimension concerns an individual's desire to climb up the corporate ladder, being recognised and rewarded appropriately as each higher level of seniority is achieved.

9. Financial Reward / Security

This concerns the degree to which an individual is driven by the need to achieve financial security and the benefits that come with it.

10. Status / Power

This dimension is about an individual's drive to be recognised for the position they have attained, and the satisfaction they achieve from being able to exert influence and power over a team, function or organisation.

Why this conversation matters

We have polled hundreds of organisations during webinars about 5 Conversations asking which of the 5 Conversations is most needed within their organisation. 'Building for the future' is the conversation that usually comes out on top. When asked why this is, leaders often report from their personal experience that this is the conversation they would most like to have personally to be sure they really understand the diverse range of career opportunities they could have access to, and that their organisation understands them and where they want to get to.

We all know that the days of a job for life are long gone. We all expect to build our careers within a number of organisations or across employed and self-employed roles during our working lives. Talking about this openly with key members of your team enables you to maximise the chances of your organisation having access to the skills and talents of your best people for as long as possible. And if through the conversation you discover that it won't be possible to satisfy the career aspirations of a key employee within your organisation, at least you now know this and can maximise their effectiveness in their remaining time with you and plan to replace them or re-organise the team.

Talent Management can be usefully defined as *"getting the most effective people into the most important jobs"*. This vital activity is not just the responsibility of your HR function, but a key part of your role as a leader. This conversation plays a critical role in enabling you to do this, matching your requirements with the career aspirations of your key people.

Why this conversation often does not happen at work

We have asked many leaders for their views about why this conversation does not happen effectively at work.

One reason is that the conversation usually sits within a Performance Management or Appraisal process. This places it in a context where there are many other distracting issues being discussed, so it fails to get the attention it deserves. Once this is pointed out, leaders often resolve to have the conversation with members of their team *outside* the Performance Management process, as a stand-alone and discrete discussion.

Another factor that gets in the way of this conversation is the process of succession planning that many organisations undertake. Typically individuals are rated on a nine-box grid (or similar) against dimensions of performance and potential, to identify those ready for promotion now, and those who may become so with development within a given period. The problem is that this process is undertaken exclusively for the company's benefit, and in most cases takes no account of the career aspirations of the people themselves. And in many cases these assessments are even kept secret from the individuals for fear that those with low ratings for performance and potential will believe they have been written off. The danger with the process is that organisations are lulled into the belief that they have "dealt with" career development and forget that the individuals themselves have a stake in it too.

Finally, the most profound reason that usually emerges is that leaders are frightened of what they might learn. They fear they will uncover career aspirations or plans that they won't be able to satisfy. They worry that this may leave them in a worse position than if they had not opened the discussion, with a team member who is now more clear than ever before that they need to leave the organisation in order to fulfil their career goals. However, once leaders discuss this fear they soon conclude that it is baseless. They agree that it is much more likely that, having held the discussion, they will gain insights into their team member's career goals that will enable their organisation to have the best chance of keeping the individual, rather than it causing them to leave.

Why this conversation works

This conversation is powerful because it enables an individual to have more influence over their own destiny, something which all of us desire and value. It is also likely to lead to greater empowerment and autonomy as career opportunities unfold that meet an individual's real needs.

One of our coaches was brought in to work with Jeff, a Managing Director in a major global accounting firm. Jeff led a team of five, which he took over when the prior, much-loved, MD had unexpectedly passed away. Jeff was appointed temporarily to fill in while the company was looking for a replacement, and was tasked to move the team forward. In addition, it was a time of change for the firm, where re-structuring was likely, and so Jeff very much had a holding position.

Jeff was conscious that he had to keep the team functional during the time of change, but he also wanted to leave a good legacy at the end of his temporary appointment. The coach asked Jeff what had worked for him in the past and heard how the old boss had mentored him, and had encouraged him to think about what he wanted for the future and what he needed to do to get there – without which, on reflection, Jeff didn't think he would have been asked to step into his role.

The team was experiencing a difficult and uncertain time, both grieving for their old boss and being unsure of the future. Jeff recognised that, despite these difficulties, it was also a time of opportunity for his team members to decide what they wanted to happen. In particular there was a bright, 'rising star' within the team, Elisabeth. Her colleagues had nicknamed her 'Superwoman'; in her early 30s, she tried to take on anything and everything and was at risk of losing focus. Encouraged by the mentoring Jeff remembered from his old boss, he decided that it was his responsibility to have discussions with Elisabeth. Over a series of conversations, Jeff discussed with her what her strengths were, what her passions were and where she wanted to be in the future. This enabled her to move out of the mindset of 'Superwoman' and instead to focus on the activities which would be of most impact for her future. Through Jeff's conversations with Elisabeth and the rest of his team, he helped them see that there was a future with the firm, even if they were going to have different jobs.

Twelve months on and the firm was re-organised. All of Jeff's team took on roles in the new organisation (which was a major benefit to the firm, given the high cost of replacing staff). Elisabeth rose to take on greater responsibilities. She saw the benefit of her discussions with Jeff, and had similar conversations with her own team, 'passing forward' the benefit. Jeff went on to retire, having left the legacy that he'd wanted to.

As our coach reflected on what had happened for Jeff, she came to two conclusions:

Don't put off having conversations about the future just because there is a lot going on. It would have been easy for Jeff and his team just to have concentrated on the here and now, particularly given the difficult situation. However, having conversations about what the rising star wanted from the future meant that she came out of that difficult period with a clear idea of what she wanted and how she might get there.

This was not just a single conversation – it can have a great cascade effect; Jeff took the role model he had seen in his old boss and used what he learnt to have similar discussions with his own team, who then in turn had conversations with their own direct reports. This cascade process meant that they could all take an active role in building their own future.

The practicalities of holding this conversation

A. Identifying *who* to have the conversation with, and *when* it will be helpful

We recommend that this conversation should be held annually with each member of your team, but outside of the formal Performance Management process.

B. Setting up the conversation and issuing an invitation

Most people welcome the opportunity to have this conversation with their leader, so issuing the invitation and setting it up will be straightforward and uncontroversial.

In terms of preparation we recommend a simple tool called the Future Focus Wheel based on the ten dimensions listed above. The tool enables a user to score where they are now on each dimension, and then where they want to get to within an agreed timeframe. This enables the discussion to focus on where the gaps are largest, and what this means in practical terms for a future role and personal development.

The Future Focus Wheel

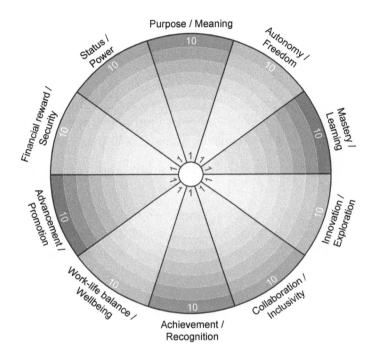

The wheel, together with instructions on how to complete it, is in the conversation toolkit at the back of this book.

C.   Planning the agenda for the conversation

We recommend that the agenda for the discussion focuses on those dimensions where the gap between where your team member is now, and where they wish to get to, is the largest, plus any other dimensions that are particularly important to them.

The key questions on each of the dimensions are:

"What's driving you to have these ambitions?"

"What opportunities can we create right now for you to move towards these goals here in this organisation?"

"What can we both do together to make this happen?"

D.   Closing

After the conversation, make a point of following up with a face-to-face chat or phone call to confirm the key insights and action points. You may also find it helpful to formalise actions you've agreed by email.

One further thought. We know of leaders who have shared their own future focus work wheel with team members as a way of building trust and respect. Even if you don't go that far, there is a lot to be gained by sharing one or two examples of things that are important to you in your future career or by describing choices and trade-offs you made on your career path to date.

In summary

Many leaders have told us this is the least held and most needed conversation in their organisation. We all think constantly about our futures. We have dreams and ambitions, hopes and fears, for what the years ahead will hold. Sometimes we share them with friends and partners, but rarely do we have the undivided attention of our boss to focus on these things. But the benefits to you of having the opportunity to do this are immense. Today's organisations are changing so rapidly that there will often be a new and exciting career path you can take, if only your manager takes the time to understand your dreams and aspirations. And organisations stand to benefit too from retaining their best people and building strength and depth in their people. As a leader there is little more fulfilling than helping people to achieve their dreams.

CHAPTER 10

Other ways to use 5 Conversations

This book is designed to enhance your confidence and capability to have different sorts of conversations with members of your team to build relationships which lead to deeper engagement. But as you were reading, were you also thinking of applications outside the manager / direct report relationship for using these powerful conversation frameworks?

Once you have become familiar with, and internalised, these conversations, you'll discover what powerful tools they are to improve relationships with all of your stakeholders – to build a culture of openness, trust and performance.

Colleagues

With colleagues your relationship is different, as there may be no element of direction, objective setting or KPI measurement. You may work with them when you take the lead on a project, or where they take the lead. You may have no direct working relationship with them at all. However, if they are a colleague then you do have a relationship with them, whatever stage it is at.

How good is it? Could it be better? Would having a great relationship with this person help you or the organisation in any way? If it would, then consider how you could use 5 Conversations in your everyday work with colleagues.

Conversation 1 – Building a trusting relationship: Informally, could you find the opportunity to work on your relationship with your colleague by opening up to them and inviting them to share information with you? Could you use this to make connections with that person? Would the risk you take in opening up to them in an appropriate way, create more trust – and would that be helpful?

Conversation 2 – Agreeing mutual expectations: If you do work jointly on some projects, developing your levels of mutual trust is essential and can then lead to successes in all five conversations. If your success relies on that person's input (or vice versa), but they do not work for you, how could you use the mutual expectations framework?

Conversation 3 – Showing genuine appreciation: Genuine appreciation, with its element of specific identified praise plus an attached emotion, will work with any colleague to improve the atmosphere, make them feel valued and make you feel good too. Can you find an opportunity to try this out?

Conversation 4 – Challenging unhelpful behaviour: Sometimes our colleagues create problems for us which, with no line management responsibility, are difficult to address. It is easy to feel that 'someone should do something about her', but if that never happens, how will it make you feel? Why not try telling the person how a specific behaviour impacted you, and how you'd like it to be in the future?

Conversation 5 – Building for the future: People often appreciate a trusted colleague acting as a sounding board as they reflect on their future. If this situation arises then suggest using the Future Focus Wheel as a helpful tool in clarifying the gaps they are seeking to close in their next career move.

Internal customers within the business

Internal customers have a difficult status where they can be critical to your success, super-critical of your failings and yet somehow tied to buying from you. This creates a challenging dynamic, causing passionate conflicts as you all seek to work towards the same ends, but with different agendas.

Conversation 1 – Building a trusting relationship: With people in other departments or divisions your relationship could be much more like a supplier/ customer relationship than that of a colleague or direct report. As such, discussing with them what drives you and what drives them can be a powerful relationship builder and totally appropriate for this relationship. Is there someone that you can think of with whom it would be helpful to develop a more trusting relationship?

Conversation 2 – Agreeing mutual expectations: Where you have an internal customer relationship then the mutual expectations conversation can be helpful in establishing a way of communicating, working together and resolving problems. You know that in such a relationship you both rely on the other person to provide, or engage with a service and to report on satisfaction with that service. Could having this conversation help you create an effective collaboration?

Conversation 3 – Showing genuine appreciation: When you are working with an internal customer, you are both technically working for the same organisation, but may have very different objectives, tasks and targets to achieve. Some of your objectives may conflict. If you can take the opportunity to identify something about them that you appreciate, would that help build your trusting relationship?

Conversation 4 – Challenging unhelpful behaviour: Conversely, if you have a problem which that person is identified with, would being able to discuss it with them be helpful? What if you could raise the issue in a safe and non-judgmental way, being very specific about behaviour and its impact on how you felt?

Conversation 5 – Building for the future: It may not be appropriate to initiate this conversation with internal customers, but again, these conversations do happen from time to time and the Future Focus Wheel structure could be helpful.

Your boss

A colleague tells us, "I am told I am good at upwards management, whereas all I really do is think about what my boss needs and what his problems are, and try to work with them in mind. I'm not afraid of pointing out that they need to change something if what they normally do does not work." Having a trusting relationship with your manager enables all sorts of issues to be raised and dealt with, without fear of criticism.

Conversation 1 – Building a trusting relationship: If your manager is new to you, or deals with you in a purely transactional way, or is simply somewhat remote, you could use the techniques in Conversation 1 to develop this into something more rewarding. If you can find an opportunity (or make one) to start the conversation about what you understand about each other, it will have a powerful transformational impact on your relationship.

Conversation 2 – Agreeing mutual expectations: In theory, your manager and you should be mutually dependent for delivering the successes that your organisation needs. If you don't find this is happening in practice, then try this conversation to understand what you could contract between you, to hold each other to account.

Conversation 3 – Showing genuine appreciation: All of us need praise and sometimes there is much attention paid to whether someone is providing positive messages to their staff, but not to whether they themselves are getting them. This conversation is a way of addressing this. Could you find something that your manager has said, done, shared or experienced that you could appreciate and talk to them about?

Conversation 4 – Challenging unhelpful behaviour: There are some occasions when it is the manager who is the problem. Instead of getting to the point where you say "Right, I am out of here", why not try the technique of letting them know how you feel, using this structured approach? One colleague tells us, "My old boss was almost universally disliked throughout the company for his displays of frustration and his nit-picking ways. Personally I found him full of good ideas and felt that the behaviour of senior members of the team towards him was almost equivalent to bullying. However he did seem to bring it on himself. We sat down one day and talked openly and honestly about this, and how his repeated displays of anger made me feel embarrassed and frustrated at what seemed to be a pointless pattern. After that the behaviour didn't change totally, but it was easier to remind him that what he was doing hadn't worked before and that he may as well try something new. Life became calmer and there were fewer opportunities for the other directors to score points."

Conversation 5 – Building for the future: Discussing your future with your boss may not be as scary as you think. Why not find the opportunity to explain to your boss what elements of your job you would like more or less of – and what you see as your own specific strengths? If you aren't sure, use the Future Focus Wheel yourself so that you know how you feel.

Yourself

While you were reading this book, did you think that you could improve your own engagement and performance by using the techniques in these conversations on yourself?

Could you need to think about these conversations with yourself: the extent to which you trust yourself, the extent to which you acknowledge the things that you do well and the things that challenge you. You can also consider the things that you do that are not helpful, as well as the extent to which you think about the future and take steps towards it.

Conversation 1 – Building a trusting relationship: How open and honest are you with yourself? How well do you trust yourself to do what you know is right? Do you find that you lack courage sometimes – and wish that you could say what you thought? Do you trust your judgement? How could you be more open about what you truly believe? Do you need to take time away from projects and tasks to think this through?

Conversation 2 – Agreeing mutual expectations: What are you passionate about and what would be a really stretching but motivating goal for you? Who can help you achieve what you want to achieve? Why does it matter to you?

Conversation 3 – Showing genuine appreciation: Do you ever take the time to acknowledge what you do really well? We often take our personal strengths for granted. One of our colleagues says, "My husband is great at high level scientific thinking but struggles to put together a formal letter – he just doesn't know how to do it. I can do it really easily, but it never occurred to me that this was a skill that someone else, someone intellectually highly capable, might not have and would value."

Conversation 4 – Challenging unhelpful behaviour: What are the traits and behaviours that you catch yourself doing, that you dislike? Could you work through to identify what the behaviour is – not in general terms, but narrowed down to specifics – then work out how it makes you feel and others feel? If you did this, might it create an opportunity to change?

Conversation 5 – Building for the future: Do you think about your future? If you have had the chance to look at your own behaviour, could you link it to deficiencies or gaps between where you are now and where you would like to be? How could you seek opportunities to bring more of what you want into your current role or another role in your organisation? Why not use the Future Focus Wheel to think about your own future career?

How can you use 5 Conversations in different types of organisations and teams?

You may be thinking that it's all very well to have 5 Conversations when you have a small team where you spend a lot of time together or when you work in an organisation where everyone is in the same location, but how does it work when you work in a more complex organisation structure?

Very large teams

If you have an exceptionally large team, it's unlikely that you will be able to have in-depth conversations with every team member. Instead, seek to identify and obtain the best possible relationship with them that you can, by doing things to enable them to know and trust you. You do have to prioritise, otherwise it's just not feasible. So whether you meet them all in a room of 200, or whether you happen to meet them once a year one-to-one, you should make it your primary objective that they understand and trust you more as a result of that interaction.

Multi-cultural teams

Working proactively to build trusting relationships is even more important where team members come from a variety of different national cultures. Having tested these conversations with colleagues and clients across the world, we have encountered no resistance to their use and we're confident that they work equally well irrespective of culture.

Indeed during a global client project we had the opportunity to survey nearly 300 consultants from more than 30 nationalities about their reaction to having authentic conversations to demonstrate trust and curiosity. Every one responded that in their own culture, showing genuine curiosity, in a spirit of learning, collaboration and building trust, was seen as a wholly positive trait and would be warmly welcomed. These conversations are not about the words you use, but rather about your genuine intention to make a connection, to be interested in the other person as a fellow human being, to reach out – which transcends any cultural differences.

Virtual and dispersed teams

It may seem like a real challenge to find opportunities to develop trusting relationships with team members when they are geographically dispersed and you rarely see them face-to-face, but our experience tells us that it *is* possible to develop trusting relationships at a distance.

Where it is not feasible or affordable to meet face-to-face we recommend three key principles to adopt to develop effective and trusting relationships at a distance:

- **Personalisation:** The corner stone in making remote relationships work remains establishing a direct link between you and each member of your team, and we have seen conversation 1 work superbly well at a distance, for example by telephone or Skype, with little adaptation. Subsequent conversations which explore and agree how each party likes to communicate and be communicated with, collaborate with others, check and report on progress, provide support and be supported, are extremely useful in agreeing a set of commitments and expectations that can be made to each other (conversation 2).

One effective technique can be to set up with each team member a 30-minute discussion each month without a set agenda, just to acknowledge and reflect on what is going on for each other at the moment and have the time and space to talk. By having such conversations with each member of your team you can develop a picture of how best to work with them. It also gives you the opportunity to express your appreciation (conversation 3) in reaction to their description of what is going on for them.

Given that conference calls are an everyday feature of dispersed teams, awareness of individual preferences can be of real value, as can small gestures such as making use of participants' names on conference calls, acknowledging things that are happening in their locality and alternating the chair of the discussion.

- **Simplification:** It's important to ensure that communications are clear, simple and unambiguous, and kept to a minimum to avoid overload, misunderstanding and distraction. This means thinking carefully about both the destination of communications (especially limiting the number of people copied in to emails) and also how much is absolutely necessary.

  In our experience, when working at a distance 'less is more'. This makes it even more important to ensure there is a regular and consistent flow of information in both directions to ensure a smooth business operation. Planning and regulating this reduces stress and uncertainty and enables other communications to be set up for exceptional or emerging topics.

  Similarly if there is a need for conversation 4, this needs to be clearly and simply set up in advance, at a convenient time and of course through live dialogue, ideally with a visual connection.

  The same principles are true for holding conversation 5.

- **Amplification:** The fact of working at a distance means that communications and meanings often need to be amplified to get through and to ensure they are understood. This means that communication efforts have to be increased and frequency and consistency are important elements.

It can be even more important to take time to show genuine appreciation when contact is infrequent and to make sure the message is received loud and clear; and why not use the opportunities presented by technology to add some colour or fun to your message?

Finally it is good to mix up communications so that they don't become too predictable, stale and uninspiring and to use different kinds of 'spaces' for different conversations. We know of some leaders who produce a weekly blog for their team and encourage comments and reactions; another uses a hand-held video camera to capture and send out short communications, encouraging his team members to do the same in response; and another who invites the team to a virtual, informal, end-of-the-week 'cocktail' session.

In summary

Re-discover the power and the joy of holding open, honest, two-way conversations, not just with members of your close team, but also with a wide range of colleagues and stakeholders. Whether you can hold these conversations face-to-face or have to rely on remote technology to connect you with others, authentic conversations where you listen with curiosity, care and humanity are what make the real difference in building long-term, productive, trusting relationships.

CHAPTER 11

Conclusion

We hope you have enjoyed reading about the 5 Conversations that can transform trust, engagement and performance at work. We believe they have the potential to change your life as a leader, not only by transforming the performance of your team, but also by enhancing your quality of life and sense of fulfilment at work and beyond.

Having trusting personal relationships around us is a deep human need. Some people seem to know this instinctively and have the knack of building them naturally with colleagues and others at work. But many people in leadership roles have forgotten (or never learnt) that this matters deeply to them too, and that it's something they can consciously work on.

We have shared our beliefs about the power of conversation to build trusting relationships with many thousands of leaders over a thirty-year period in countries around the globe. We have engaged in countless deep and animated discussions as leaders have articulated and tested their own assumptions and beliefs about people, teams and performance at work. The overwhelming majority have concluded that the voluntary commitment of the people in their own teams and organisations is a fundamental driver of organisational success. They have recognised that they have a role as leaders in building this commitment and that the 5 Conversations give them, perhaps for the first time, a set of practical tools they can use to achieve this. When we have contacted them six months and a year later, the results for many of them have been remarkable and transformational.

They report that appreciating the power of honest, face-to-face conversations has been a profound learning experience with a positive impact not just within the work environment but also outside work and in their home lives. They describe how their time efficiency has improved at work and how the spirit, morale and engagement of their teams have improved. They proudly relate concrete examples of challenging conversations they have planned for and held, and the positive outcomes they have achieved. And best of all they give hard examples of improvements in organisational and business performance that they attribute directly to holding these conversations with an authentic intention to listen, to understand and to support.

It is sometimes said that holding conversations at work contributes little to the hard financial realities of business performance. Surely *real* business leaders focus on customers, sales, innovation, efficiency and reporting? Well, of course they do. But the *best* business leaders know that this is not enough. They know that without the whole-hearted and genuine engagement of their *people*, little of lasting and sustainable value can be created. As a result they not only have the engagement of their people firmly on their radar as a key business metric, but they also walk the talk and expect every leader in their organisation to do the same. They know that the web of informal, trusting relationships across their organisation is really what gets results, and they work tirelessly to build and reinforce it.

The CEO of a global manufacturing organisation told us this story:

We received an enquiry recently in Spain for the supply of a massive order of specialist bearings. We don't have the technical capacity in Europe to manufacture this type of bearing. Because of the relationship the country manager had built with his counterpart in the US he called him personally and asked if he could take on the order. The US guy said "yes" so we supplied them from the US instead. The country manager in Spain didn't get any financial recognition in his P&L for this but did it because he's forged a personal bond with his colleague in the US through your programme.

I can tell you that three years ago this would *never* have happened. The personal relationships leaders are building within their teams, between themselves, and with all of us on the ExCom are transforming the performance of this business.

We opened this book calling for a new era of relationship-based leadership. We believe profoundly that in today's world of work we need to re-discover the power of authentic *human* connections in getting things done. No one can turn back the clock on our new world of 24/7 virtual interactions through email, social media and the web and we wouldn't want to. This is our new reality and the world is a more exciting, dynamic and vibrant place for it.

But we do profoundly believe that our world of digital connection can never be a substitute for face-to-face human contact. The more deeply we enter a world of electronic connections, the more essential it is to reach out at a human level to build authentic, emotional connections based on two-way, face-to-face conversation.

On our workshops leaders try out the conversations face-to-face, with colleagues and team members, and feel their power at first hand. We hope that reading this book has provided an alternative route into these conversations and that as a result you too will be inspired to try them out and feel their power.

We would love to hear about your experiences in doing this, so please go to www.5conversations.co.uk and tell us about your success and learning so we can share this with others who are on the same journey.

APPENDIX

Conversation Toolkits

In this book we've taken you through each of the 5 Conversations and given you examples of how people have used them as well as a step-by-step guide of how to approach each conversation. We've taken the guidance from each conversation to produce these conversation toolkits: practical planners and checklists you can use to help you put the conversations into action.

For each conversation, we've included a conversation planner. This takes you through the process of planning for the conversation, giving you prompts for each stage in the process. It encourages you to be clear about who you want to have the conversation with and why. It then asks you to plan an agenda for the conversation, and reminds you of what you need to do in closing the conversation and then following it up. For some of the conversations we've provided a list of questions that you may find helpful in planning the conversation.

In the case of conversation 4 (challenging unhelpful behaviour) we've included the inventory of feelings and needs developed by the Center for Nonviolent Communication, to give you a vocabulary for what you may want to say.

For conversation 5 (building for the future) there is a copy of the Future Focus Wheel, and instructions on how to complete it.

You can download a copy of these planners from our website, www.5conversations.co.uk, ready to use the next time you are preparing to have one of the conversations.

Try them out and have those conversations!

Conversation 1 – Establishing a trusting relationship

Conversation Planner

STAGES IN THE CONVERSATION	MY NOTES
Setting up & issuing invitation	
Who do I want to have the conversation with?	
Why will building a deeper relationship benefit us both and the business?	
How will I word the invitation?	
Preparing myself: • Am I clear about why this conversation will be of benefit? • Have I thought through the agenda and questions? • What are my intentions and motivations – do I have a genuine desire to develop a more trusting relationship?	

Agenda and questions	
Opening question (encourage them to ask it to you as well)	What would you most like to ask me that will help you to understand me better?
What other questions do I want to ask?	

Closing and following up	
Closing	How did you find the conversation? I feel I have gained… in terms of building a better relationship with you Thank you
Following up: • What is the best way of following up (face-to-face? phone call?) • This isn't a one-off – when would it next be helpful to find out more about your colleague?	

Potential Questions

Opening question	What would you most like to ask me that will help you to understand me better?
Questions which reveal what they value	What's really important to you at work? What do you feel most strongly about? What are you most passionate about?
Questions which indicate how they view themselves	What do you consider your greatest strength? What are you most proud of? What do you think is your greatest limitation? What do you want to be known for? What is it that you really stand for?

Questions which show what's important to them in their relationships with others	What's important to you in building a relationship with someone?
	What matters most to you when trusting others?
	When do you tend to feel most badly let down by a colleague?
	What sorts of things destroy a relationship for you?
	To what extent do you tend to open up to others at work?
	How easily do you trust others?
	What one thing could I tell you that would help you to trust me?
Questions which highlight what they need from work	Tell me about a good day at work?
	What gives you most satisfaction at work?
	What energises you?
	Tell me what a bad day at work looks like?
	What causes you most anxiety at work?
	What causes you to lose sleep at night?
	Which emotions do you experience most often?

Open question once you've both revealed more in response to specific questions	What one question could I ask you that would enable me to really understand you?
Questions when you know the other person well	What one thing can you tell me that might be helpful for me to know about you that I don't already know? Do you have any unrealised ambitions? What do you most value about working here? What one thing would you change about working here and why? What would you like to be most remembered for?

Conversation 2 – Agreeing mutual expectations

Conversation Planner

STAGES IN THE CONVERSATION	MY NOTES
Setting up & issuing invitation	
What is my sense of purpose?	Which parts of my job make me feel most fulfilled? What do I want my legacy at work to be? How do I want to be remembered if I left? Which goals do I feel most passionate about? What is driving me towards them?
Who do I want to have the conversation with?	
Why will it be useful for us to agree mutual expectations? In what specific area/s do we need to agree expectations?	
How will I word the invitation?	

Preparing myself: • Am I clear about why this conversation will be of benefit and how we are mutually dependent? • Have I thought through the agenda and questions? • How am I going to express my purpose in way that is authentic for me?	
Agenda and questions	
Opening question	
What other questions do I want to ask?	

Closing and following up	
Closing	How did you find the conversation? I feel I have gained… in terms of getting a clear understanding of what we're both trying to achieve and our expectations of each other Thank you
Following up: • What is the best way of following up (face-to-face? phone call?) • Summarise any specific actions agreed • Carry out the actions!	

Potential Questions

Let me give you an overview of what I'm trying to achieve over the next period, and especially why this matters for me …

Can you talk me through the same thing from your point of view? What are you trying to achieve and why is it important to you?

So can we explore how we can support each other in achieving our goals?

How can I support you in terms of resources, influencing, coaching, etc.? What would be most helpful for you?

How do you think you can best support me?

How might we get in each other's way? Is there anything we should be aware of or avoid doing?

So can we summarise the expectations we have of each other, and how we can hold each other to account for delivering on these expectations?

Conversation 3 – Showing genuine appreciation

Conversation Planner

STAGES IN THE CONVERSATION	MY NOTES
Setting up & issuing invitation	
Who do I want to have the conversation with?	
What have they done that I want to recognise and show appreciation?	
How will I word the invitation?	
Preparing myself: • Am I clear about what I want to show appreciation for? • What words do I want to use to express my appreciation? • How can I show my feelings and make my appreciation genuine?	

Agenda and questions	
Questions to understand and appreciate what's going on	
Questions to explore how to build on this good work	
Questions to consolidate what could happen next	
Closing and following up	
Closing	Thank you
Following up: • What is the best way of following up (face-to-face? phone call?) • Repeat thanks for what they have done • Summarise any specific actions agreed • Carry out the actions!	

Potential Questions

Understand and appreciate	What's going really well for you at the moment?
	What's been your biggest success in the last few weeks?
	What's been your biggest achievement recently?
	What's been your biggest challenge?
	What was the situation?
	What were the key challenges you faced?
	What did you say and do that led to success?
	How did you feel as this was happening?
	What strengths, talents and skills of yours contributed most to this outcome?
	What's the learning you take from this experience?
	How are you feeling right now?
	Thank You! I want you to know that I really appreciate the contribution you are making, and the skills and commitment you are bringing to our team

Explore	What other opportunities are there for you to use these strengths, talents and skills?
	How else can we play to your strengths?
	How do you want to develop these skills further?
Consolidate	What's the key insight you have gained from this discussion?
	What learning points should we both take away?
	What are the action points that we both commit to follow up on?

Conversation 4 – Challenging unhelpful behaviour

Conversation Planner

STAGES IN THE CONVERSATION	MY NOTES
Setting up & issuing invitation	
Who do I want to have the conversation with?	
When will it be helpful to have it?	
How will I word the invitation?	
Preparing myself: • Am I clear about what behaviour I want to challenge? • Have I thought through the agenda and questions? • What are my intentions and motivations – why do I want to do this?	

Agenda and questions	
Observations: what have I observed?	My observations: What is your perspective on the situation?
Feelings: how did it make me / others feel?	My feelings: How were you feeling and why?
Needs: what do I need?	My needs: What needs are important to you?
Requests: what am I asking them to do?	My requests: Do you have any requests of me?

Closing and following up	
Closing	'Re-boot': check in and reconnect Thank you
Following up	Show genuine appreciation at a positive shift in behaviour

Feelings Inventory

The following are words we use when we want to express a combination of emotional states and physical sensations. This list is neither exhaustive nor definitive. It is meant as a starting place to support anyone who wishes to engage in a process of deepening self-discovery and to facilitate greater understanding and connection between people. There are two parts to this list: feelings we may have when our needs are being met and feelings we may have when our needs are not being met.

Feelings when your needs are satisfied

AFFECTIONATE
compassionate
friendly
loving
open hearted
sympathetic
tender
warm

ENGAGED
absorbed
alert
curious
engrossed
enchanted
entranced
fascinated
interested
intrigued

involved
spellbound
stimulated

HOPEFUL
expectant
encouraged
optimistic

CONFIDENT
empowered
open
proud
safe
secure

EXCITED
amazed
animated

ardent
aroused
astonished
dazzled
eager
energetic
enthusiastic
giddy
invigorated
lively
passionate
surprised
vibrant

GRATEFUL
appreciative
moved
thankful
touched

INSPIRED
amazed
awed
wonder

JOYFUL
amused
delighted
glad
happy
jubilant
pleased
tickled

EXHILARATED
blissful
ecstatic

elated
enthralled
exuberant
radiant
rapturous
thrilled

PEACEFUL
calm
clear headed
comfortable
centered
content
equanimous
fulfilled
mellow
quiet

relaxed
relieved
satisfied
serene
still
tranquil
trusting

REFRESHED
enlivened
rejuvenated
renewed
rested
restored
revived

Feelings when your needs are not satisfied

AFRAID
apprehensive
dread
foreboding
frightened
mistrustful
panicked
petrified
scared
suspicious
terrified
wary
worried

ANNOYED
aggravated
dismayed
disgruntled
displeased
exasperated
frustrated
impatient
irritated
irked

ANGRY
enraged

furious
incensed
indignant
irate
livid
outraged
resentful

AVERSION
animosity
appalled
contempt
disgusted

dislike
hate
horrified
hostile
repulsed

CONFUSED
ambivalent
baffled
bewildered
dazed
hesitant
lost
mystified
perplexed
puzzled
torn

DISCONNECTED
alienated
aloof
apathetic
bored
cold
detached
distant
distracted
indifferent
numb
removed
uninterested
withdrawn

DISQUIET
agitated
alarmed
discombobulated
disconcerted
disturbed
perturbed
rattled
restless
shocked
startled
surprised
troubled
turbulent
turmoil
uncomfortable
uneasy
unnerved
unsettled
upset

EMBARRASSED
ashamed
chagrined
flustered
guilty
mortified
self-conscious

FATIGUE
beat
burnt out
depleted
exhausted
lethargic

listless
sleepy
tired
weary
worn out

PAIN
agony
anguished
bereaved
devastated
grief
heartbroken
hurt
lonely
miserable
regretful
remorseful

SAD
depressed
dejected
despair
despondent
disappointed
discouraged
disheartened
forlorn
gloomy
heavy hearted
hopeless
melancholy
unhappy
wretched

TENSE
anxious
cranky
distressed
distraught
edgy
fidgety
frazzled
irritable
jittery
nervous

overwhelmed
restless
stressed out

VULNERABLE
fragile
guarded
helpless
insecure
leery
reserved

sensitive
shaky

YEARNING
envious
jealous
longing
nostalgic
pining
wistful

Needs Inventory

The following list of needs is neither exhaustive nor definitive. It is meant as a starting place to support anyone who wishes to engage in a process of deepening self-discovery and to facilitate greater understanding and connection between people.

CONNECTION

acceptance
affection
appreciation
belonging
cooperation
communication
closeness
community
companionship
compassion
consideration
consistency
empathy
inclusion
intimacy
love
mutuality
nurturing
respect/self-respect
safety
security
stability
support
to know and be known
to see and be seen
to understand and be understood
trust
warmth

PHYSICAL WELL-BEING

air
food
movement/exercise
rest/sleep
sexual expression
safety
shelter
touch
water

HONESTY

authenticity
integrity
presence

PLAY

joy
humor

PEACE

beauty
communion
ease
equality
harmony
inspiration
order

AUTONOMY

choice
freedom
independence
space
spontaneity

MEANING

awareness
celebration of life
challenge
clarity
competence
consciousness
contribution
creativity
discovery

efficacy	learning	self-expression
effectiveness	mourning	stimulation
growth	participation	to matter
hope	purpose	understanding

Conversation 5 – Building for the future

Conversation Planner

STAGES IN THE CONVERSATION	MY NOTES
Setting up & issuing invitation	
Who do I want to have the conversation with?	
When will it be helpful to have it?	
How will I word the invitation? Is there any preparation I would like them to do (e.g. complete the Future Focus Wheel)?	
Preparing myself: • Am I clear about why this conversation will be of benefit? • Have I thought through the agenda and questions? • What are my intentions and motivations – do I have a genuine desire to act on the outcomes of the discussion?	

Agenda and questions	
Deciding the focus of the conversation	Which are the dimensions on the wheel where the gap between where you are now and where you want to get to is the largest?
	Are there any other dimensions which are particularly important to you?
For each dimension discussed	What's driving you to have these ambitions?
	What opportunities can we create right now for you to move towards these goals here in this organisation?
	What can we both do together to make this happen?
Closing and following up	
Closing	How did you find the conversation?
	Summary of key insights and action points
	Thank you

Following up:	
• What is the best way of following up (face-to-face? phone call?)	
• Summary of key insights and action points	
• Carry out the actions!	

Future Focus Wheel

The Future Focus wheel measures how you currently see yourself in your job and where you would like to be in the future against ten different dimensions:

- Purpose / Meaning: the extent to which you need to have a clear line of sight between your own role and a greater goal

- Autonomy / Freedom: the extent to which you need a high degree of freedom to act and control over your own job content and the ability to shape the future of your team / function / business

- Mastery / Learning: the extent to which you need a role which requires mastery of knowledge / skills and continuous development of these

- Innovation / Exploration: the extent to which you need your role to provide opportunities for creativity, discovery, innovation and exploration

- Collaboration / Inclusivity: the extent to which your role allows you to work closely with other people

- Achievement / Recognition: the extent to which your role allows you to win, succeed and achieve and be recognised and rewarded for doing so

- Work-Life Balance / Wellbeing: the extent to which you are able to balance your time and effort at work with a life outside work, and the extent to which you can meet your needs for your own physical, mental and emotional state.

- Advancement / Promotion: the extent to which your role allows you to advance and be promoted

- Financial Reward / Security: the extent to which your role provides you with the financial reward and security you need

- Status / Power: the extent to which your role gives you the status you wish and the level of influence and power over others

To complete the wheel:

1. Take each dimension in turn and make a mark on the scale between 1 and 10 (where 1 is "very dissatisfied" and 10 is "totally satisfied") to indicate where you feel you are now in your career. Now join up each of these marks.

2. Next, work through each of the same dimensions and make another mark between 1 and 10 to indicate where you want to be within a given timeframe (for example 3 years). Again join up each of these marks.

3. Now reflect on the shape of the two spidergrams you have created and ask yourself what it tells you about the career development steps and opportunities you need to seek. Firstly, which of the dimensions are most important to you? These may be priorities for action, even if the gap between where you are now, and where you

want to be, is small. Next look at the dimensions where the gaps are largest. These too may be areas for action.

My Future Focus Wheel

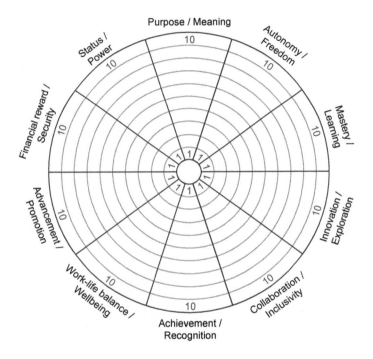

Bibliography

1. Collins, J. (2001). *Good to Great.* New York: Collins Business

2. Ryde, R. (2012). *Never Mind the Bosses: Hastening the Death of Deference for Business Success.* London: John Wiley & Sons

3. Gallup, Inc. (2013). *State of the Global Workplace – Employee engagement insights for business leaders worldwide.* Gallup, Inc.

4. Groysberg, B. & Slind, M. (2012). *Leadership is a conversation.* Harvard Business Review, June 2012

5. MacLeod, D. & Clarke, N. (2009). *Engaging for Success: enhancing performance through employee engagement.* Crown Copyright

6. Rayton, B., Dodge, T. & D'Analeze, G. (2012). *The Evidence: Employee Engagement Taskforce, "Nailing the Evidence" Workgroup.* Engage for Success

7. Aon Hewitt. (2012). *Trends in Global Employee Engagement.* Aon Corporation

8. Harter, James K., Schmidt, F.L., Killham, E.A. and Agrawal, S. (2012). *Q12® Meta-Analysis: The Relationship between Engagement at Work and Organizational Outcomes.* Gallup, Inc.

9. Royal, M. & Stark, M. (2010). *Hitting the ground running, what the world's most admired companies do to (re)engage their employees.* The Hay Group

10. Wiley, J. (2009). *Driving Success through Performance Excellence and Employee Engagement.* Kenexa Research Institute

11. Towers Watson. (2012). *2012 Global Workforce Study.* Towers Watson

12. Kenexa. (2012). *Kenexa WorkTrends Survey.* IBM

13. Atkinson, S. & Butcher, D. (2003). *Trust in managerial relationships.* Journal of Managerial Psychology, Vol. 18, No. 4, pp. 282-304

14. Çerri, S. (2012*). Exploring factors affecting trust and relationship quality in a supply chain context.* Journal of Business Studies Quarterly 2012, Vol. 4, No. 1, pp. 74-90

15. MacLean, P.D. (1990). *The Triune Brain in Evolution: Role in Paleocerebral Functions.* New York: Plenum Press

16. Pinker, S. (1997). *How the mind works.* New York: W W Norton & Co Inc.

17. Goleman, D. (1995). *Emotional Intelligence: Why it Can Matter More Than IQ.* New York: Bantam Books Inc.

18. Brown, P. & Hales, B. (2011). *Neuroscience – New Science for New Leadership.* Developing Leaders, 2011, Issue 5

19. Maister, D.H., Green, C.H. & Galford, R.M. (2000). *The Trusted Advisor.* New York: Free Press

20. Pink, D.H. (2009). *Drive: The Surprising Truth About What Motivates Us.* New York: Riverhead Hardcover

21. Sinek, S. (2009). *Start With Why: How Great Leaders Inspire Everyone To Take Action.* New York: Portfolio Hardcover

22. Covey, Stephen M.R. (2006). *The Speed of Trust: The One Thing That Changes Everything.* New York: Free Press

23. Cooperrider, D.L. & Srivastva, S. (1987). *Appreciative inquiry in organizational life.* Research in organizational change and development, volume 1, pp. 129-169

24. Rosenberg, M. (2001). *Nonviolent Communication: a Language of Life.* Encinitas, CA: Puddle Dancer Press

25. Rock, D. (2008). *SCARF: a brain-based model for collaborating with and influencing others.* Neuroleadership Journal, Issue 1, pp. 78-87

About the authors

Nick Cowley

This is Nick's first book and has been an opportunity to draw on his wealth of management experience in major corporations. Before joining The Oxford Group in 1994, his career included roles with British Airways, Bayer AG and Whitbread in operational management, HR and OD across Europe and the Middle East. Nick gained particular corporate expertise in leading international projects, participating in merger and acquisition activity and significant organisational change programmes, as well as designing and implementing learning and development architecture. As a Director of The Oxford Group, he has a particular responsibility for acquiring and growing client relationships over the long term. He also leads the development of our Management Development services and works as an Executive Coach. In 2013, Nick led the development of The Oxford Group's 5 Conversations programme, the concept from which this book was created.

Linked in. uk.linkedin.com/in/nickcowley

Nigel Purse

Nigel is an experienced facilitator, writer and speaker whose passion lies in developing management and leadership capability in both new and senior leaders in organisations worldwide. He is Chairman and Director of The Oxford Group, which he co-founded in 1987 following a career in HR and business management  with the Mars Corporation and Burmah Oil. Under Nigel's leadership The Oxford Group has grown from its roots as a small company specialising in behavioural assessment to a global consultancy providing leadership and management development as well as executive coaching. Believing in the importance of employees being engaged with the values of their organisation, he also remains personally involved in the recruitment, induction and development of new Oxford Group consultants worldwide. In 2013, Nigel was instrumental in the development and launch of the 5 Conversations programme.

Linked in. uk.linkedin.com/in/nigelpurse

THE Oxford Group

The Oxford Group is a global organisation, providing management training, leadership development and executive coaching to the world's leading companies since 1987. Its consultants work with clients as partners to develop bespoke, world-class solutions that are practical and impactful, and deliver these on a global scale to all levels of leaders. As a learning and development provider, its strength lies in taking a blended approach to training, combining extensive expertise in face-to-face delivery with a range of technology-based methods, to provide participants with a complete learning journey. Most importantly, The Oxford Group's work is based on a belief that people come to work wanting to do a good job, and that everyone has huge, untapped reserves of creativity and potential - the role of its consultants is to unlock that potential by engaging participants with techniques, exercises and content that are stimulating and relevant to them.